Please return to

Grace by
William Pierce Stubbs

PLAY AS YOU LEARN BRIDGE

BY Charles H. Goren

GOREN'S BRIDGE COMPLETE

GOREN'S NEW CONTRACT BRIDGE COMPLETE

CONTRACT BRIDGE COMPLETE

POINT COUNT BIDDING MADE EASY: A SELF-TEACHER

CONTRACT BRIDGE IN A NUTSHELL

THE STANDARD BOOK OF BIDDING

BETTER BRIDGE FOR BETTER PLAYERS

THE PRECISION SYSTEM OF CONTRACT BRIDGE BIDDING

GOREN ON PLAY AND DEFENSE

100 CHALLENGING BRIDGE HANDS

GOREN'S MODERN BACKGAMMON COMPLETE

PLAY AS
YOU LEARN
BRIDGE

A *Chancellor Hall* BOOK *published by*

DOUBLEDAY AND COMPANY, NEW YORK

DESIGNED AND PRODUCED BY CHANCELLOR HALL
Composed and printed in the United States
of America by The Book Press
Cover design by Carlos Mercado

DEDICATION
To
Harold A. Ogust,
my long-time friend, teammate and business
associate,
whose untimely death in 1978
is mourned by me and the thousands who
knew him.

INTRODUCTION

The trouble with most beginner's bridge books is that they don't begin at the beginning.

This one is different. By the time you have read the first few pages, you are actually playing a game that is fun.

This game, or something like it, is nearly five hundred years old. It is the game from which Whist, Auction Bridge and Contract Bridge developed. If you never get beyond the first two lessons of this book, you will be playing and understanding a game from which evolved – some four hundred years later – the world's best and most popular card game: Contract Bridge.

Of course, you won't want to stop there. Within the few pages of this book, you will master, in about a dozen lessons, the developments of over four centuries. Very soon, you'll be playing Contract Bridge and, even more important, you will understand the basic principles that will make you a better player right from the start. Meanwhile, I promise that you'll enjoy this "play-as-you-learn" method.

So here we are. Let's get going.

Charles H. Goren

TABLE OF CONTENTS

ACKNOWLEDGEMENTS

I must express my sincere thanks to the Goren Editorial Board, especially its chairman, Richard L. Frey, and my close associate, Tannah Hirsch, and to a new aide, August Boehm, who have contributed in large measure to the creation of this book.

PLAY AS YOU LEARN BRIDGE

Lesson 1 : getting started

LOGICALLY, the easiest way to learn – and the most fun – is to start playing at once the basic form of a game. All you need is a pack of cards, (preferably two packs but not necessarily)*, four players, a table and a pad and pencil to keep score. For the purpose of learning, however, you may deal the hands face up and play alone.

THE CARDS: The regular 52 card pack (without jokers) is composed of thirteen cards of each of four suits: Spades (♠), Hearts (♡), Diamonds (♢) and Clubs (♣). The cards of each suit rank Ace (highest), King, Queen, Jack, 10, 9, etc., down to the 2 (lowest).

THE PLAYERS: The four players form two partnerships. The players sitting across from each other are partners against the other two. You may play as you happen to be seated, or if two players prefer always to play together (called a "set game") they may do so if the opponents agree. Otherwise, partners are determined by:

THE DRAW: Shuffle the pack and spread it face down on the table. Each player draws a card. The players drawing the

*You play with only one pack at a time, but it speeds the game if a second pack is shuffled and ready while the deal is being completed.

3

two highest cards play as partners. Ties if more than one player draws a card of the same rank (eg. ♠K, ♡K) are broken by the rank of the suit: spades (high), hearts, diamonds, clubs (low).

Highest card is first to deal. (The player who draws it also has the right to choose his seat and the deck with which he will deal – a gesture toward superstition, but also a rule that settles any possible argument.) The player seated to his left shuffles the cards; the player to dealer's right cuts them, dividing the deck into two parts. Dealer completes the cut by stacking the former lower half to the top and is then ready to deal.

THE DEAL: Starting with the player at his left and proceeding clockwise, the dealer places before each player in turn the top card of the pack. It is customary for no player to pick up any cards until all the cards are dealt. When the cards are correctly dealt, the dealer receives the last card and each player has received a hand of thirteen cards. Each then picks up his *hand* (the 13 cards he has been dealt) and assorts them into suits. The player will find it most convenient to place the cards in suits, alternating red and black, and by rank, high card at the left, within the suit.

The object of the game is to win seven or more *tricks,* tricks won by either partner counting for his side. A trick consists of four cards played clockwise in order.

Starting to play

You are now ready to play the basic game that was the forerunner of whist. Although the player facing you is your partner and the tricks each takes are counted together for your side, you cannot as yet actually see what he holds. To practice all by yourself, turn all four hands face up and try to play to the best advantage of each player. Thus you will, from the very beginning and without assistance, actually play as you learn. Even if there are other players present, you might well play a couple of deals in this fashion before you engage in real trick-winning battles.

Later, you will see how one of the four hands (the dummy) is turned face up, but for the moment we are playing as if no cards but your own can be seen until they are played.

The play begins when the player to dealer's left places any card face up on the table. He may choose any card in his hand, but the other three players must then play a card of the same suit. Each may play any card of that suit as he chooses. If he has none of the suit led, he may *discard* any other card he chooses. The highest card of the suit led wins the trick. A *discard*, even if it is higher than any card played, cannot win a trick. When all four players have contributed a card in turn, the trick is complete.

Winning tricks

Here are some examples of how tricks are won:

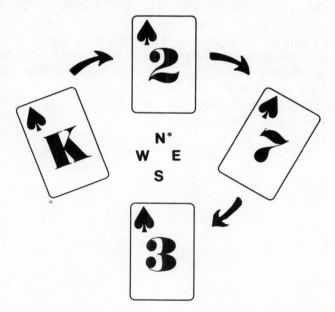

(*The initials W, N, E, S, stand for West, North, East and South. They have no relation to compass direction but are merely to designate the four players.)

The King of spades is the highest spade card on that trick, so West is the winner of the trick and leads a card to start the next trick.

The trick could have been taken away from West only if someone played the Ace of spades. Assuming that one of the other players had no spades, he could not have won the trick by playing any other ace.

If West does not have the Ace of spades in his own hand, he might assume that East, his partner, has the Ace. One reason why East would not play the Ace and win the trick is that his side is already sure of winning it; remember, a trick won by either partner counts for both.

If West has the Queen of spades along with a number of others, he might next lead a low spade, allowing East to win the second trick with the Ace. Then, if East has a third spade, he will lead it back to allow his partner to win the next trick with the spade Queen.

Let us suppose that all four players have followed to the first three spade tricks. West can now lead the 4 of spades, and it will win the fourth trick since nobody else will have a spade to play. It is important to count the number of cards that have already been played in a suit, so you will know if a low one remaining in your hand is now high.

Suppose, however, that South held the Ace of spades. The first trick would now look like this.

South has won the trick. He now has the right to lead to the next trick, and may select any card of any suit. It is not necessary for him to lead another spade.

Suppose that, instead of the King of spades, West's lead to the first trick was the Jack of spades. When it came time for South to play, the trick looked like this:

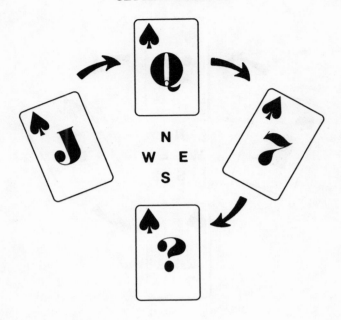

North's Queen of spades is high. If South has the Ace of spades, it is not necessary for him to play it because North has already won the trick for his side. Usually, it will be best to let North's Queen of spades hold, and South should play a low spade if he has one. (Of course if the Ace is the only spade he holds, he has no choice but to play it.) If South plays a low spade, North will have won the trick and he will lead to the next trick.

But suppose that South has a long suit of his own that he can run. He may elect to overtake his partner's trick with the King or Ace – even though it already belongs to his side – in order to be able to lead the suit he wants to cash or to establish. For example, South may have a good club suit:

Or he may have:

In the first case, he will want to have the lead so he can run off his suit. With the second holding, he may wish to force out the Ace of clubs while he still has a high spade with which he hopes to regain the lead later.

In this case, it is probably right for him to win his partner's trick in order that he, not North, shall lead to the next trick. This is especially true if South has the King of spades as well as the Ace because if he lets North's Queen win the trick it will be unlikely that North will choose to lead a club.

Now let us assume a different first lead. This time the first two plays are:

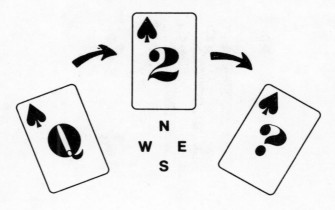

East has the Ace of spades and two lower ones. He can win the Ace and lead back the suit. OR he can play his higher card below the Ace to tell partner he has something in the suit. There are two possible advantages to this.   **1]** North may have the King of spades, even though he did not play it. In that case, West's Queen of spades will win the trick. Or   **2]** if South holds the King of spades, he will be able to win the first trick but when next East or West wins a trick, if a spade is led East will be able to win the trick with the Ace and still have a low one to get back to partner's Jack. (However, if East has only two spades in his hand, he should take his Ace and lead back his low one.)

How does East know that his partner has the Jack of spades? Well, presumably when he chose his lead, it was with the idea of establishing tricks in his suit. He might choose a suit because he has five or six cards in it, and he hopes that, with partner's help or because the opponents are short in his suit, he will drive out the high cards and win tricks with long cards. This assumes he can regain the lead after no one else has any spades remaining. So, although he may have high cards in other suits, he plays his long suit first and saves his high cards to regain the lead later.

Suppose he had five spades headed by the Queen but not including the Jack. He should lead a low card and keep the

Queen until the Ace and King of spades have already been played.

You have just learned two important principles of how to play: 1] lead your long suit first; 2] do not lead unsupported high cards at the beginning.

Since West chose to lead the Queen, he should therefore have the Jack and perhaps the ten as well. And he probably began with at least four cards of the suit he has led; otherwise, by leading spades, he would help someone else to establish long-card tricks.

A third principle also becomes clear. When the leader's partner wins a trick, it is usually desirable for him to return the lead of partner's suit unless he clearly has a better and more surely establishable suit of his own. Co-operation between partners is one of the best ways to win more tricks. Bridge is a partnership game.

Thus far we have seen that only the highest card of the suit that is led can win a trick. In other words you are playing without a trump suit or, as it is called, "notrump." But tricks can also be won by trumping, as you will learn in the next chapter.

Some rules of play

Well, let us see how much we have learned in such a short time. The leader should try to establish tricks in his long suit as soon as possible. When he holds touching cards of the suit he wants to lead (K-Q-J, Q-J-10 for example), he should lead the highest one, so that partner will know leader's strength in the suit he has led. The opening leader should not lay down aces unless he has a long suit that he expects to establish, and enough high cards to be reasonably sure of being able to lead the suit again and establish his long cards as eventual tricks. In short suits, Aces and Kings should be held to capture enemy honor cards, not led in order to capture early tricks. It does not matter which side wins the first trick. The object is to win the most tricks for your side when the deal has ended.

Here are some general rules. These are not LAWS; they are

only methods arrived at by experience, by which you will win more tricks more often:

Don't lead high cards unless they are part of a sequence. If you have a long suit you are trying to establish, lead a low card – usually the fourth highest card you hold in that suit.

Play second-hand low (unless you have all the top cards of the suit). It is usually unwise to commit your high cards to a trick before your opponents have been forced to expend their high cards.

When partner leads a low card, play third-hand high. When partner leads a low card in a suit, he is trying to promote his high cards into winning tricks by forcing out the opponents' high cards. By going up with your high card, you force the opponent to play an even higher one to win the trick, and so help your partner achieve his objective.

Usually, when you win a trick, return the suit partner has led. If you have a long suit to run, or to establish, try to win a trick as soon as possible, so that you can lead your own strong suit. Don't try to win a particular trick; try to play so that your side will win the most tricks before the deal is over.

The tricks won by each side are kept by one of the partners — usually the player who wins the first trick for his side. The four cards that comprise each trick are stacked neatly in a single unit. When a second trick has been won, it helps to keep each trick separate by placing a trick won overlapping the last one, like this:

Since there are thirteen cards in each hand, one side is sure to win the seventh, or odd trick. When your side has won six tricks, you are said to have your "book." Each trick after that counts toward your score. For convenience in keeping track, when you have won six tricks it is proper to stack the tricks you have won into a book, thereafter arranging the odd tricks in a stack as before.

Before dealing with new material, try the following quiz. The quizzes in this book are designed not only to test you, but to help you understand each lesson. Take ten points for every correct answer; don't be satisfied with less than 90%. If you score below that figure, read the lesson again. Learning bridge is like a learning a new language; you must master the basic grammar and vocabulary if the rest is to make sense.

Quiz No. 1

Starting with this quiz and for the remainder of the book, instead of using pictures of the cards we will use standard bridge notation. ♠ **A** means the Ace of spades, ♡ **8** indicates the eight of hearts. The symbols for diamonds and clubs are ♢ and ♣.

REMINDER:

1] West leads the ♢ **5**, North plays the ♢ **8**, East the ♢ **A**, South the ♢ **Q**. Which player wins the trick?

2] North leads the ♣ **J**, East the ♣ **K**, South the ♣ **4**, West the ♡ **A**. Who wins this trick?

3] If the opening lead is won by the East player, who plays first to the next trick?

4] If you hold ♠ **Q J 10 5**, which card should you lead?

5] If you hold ♡ **K J 8 6 4**, which card should you lead?

6] If you hold ♢ **A 10 5 3**, is the Ace lead good or bad?

7] If you hold ♣ **K 9 7**, is the King lead good or bad?

8] You are East and hold ♠ K 8 7 5, West (your partner) leads the ♠ J, North plays the ♠ Q and now it's your turn. Which card do you play?

9] You are South and hold ◇ A 7 2. North (partner) leads the ◇ K, East plays the five. Which card do you play?

10] You are North and hold ♡ A 5 4 3. West leads the ♡ 10. What do you play?

Answers to Quiz No. 1

1] **East.** The Ace is the highest ranking card in a suit.

2] **East.** Of all the players who *followed suit,* East played the highest card.

3] Again, **East.** The player who wins a trick begins the next one.

4] ♠ **Q.** Holding a *sequence,* lead the highest card of that sequence.

5] ♡ **6.** Holding a long broken suit, lead the *fourth best.*

6] **Bad.** It is usually poor policy to lead *unsupported honors.* If you lead the Ace you will collect only low cards from the opponents. Save the Ace to capture their honor cards and regain the lead.

7] **Bad.** For the same reasons as the previous problem.

8] ♠ **K.** The principle is *third hand high.* Even if your King loses to the Ace, by covering an opponent's honor (Queen) you will promote partner's presumed ten (remember he should lead the top of a sequence) into a trick and next time spades are lead.

9] **A low** ◇. Take 5 points extra credit for playing the seven, an encouraging card. The main thing is not to play the Ace. Partner's King will win the trick for your side.

10] ♡ **3.** The principle is *second hand low.* For all you know partner may be ready to win this trick. Then you still have the Ace to win a later trick.

Lesson 2: playing with a trump suit

THE PLAY PRINCIPLES we have discussed were formulated during the days of whist, the ancestor of modern bridge. They are still valid today. The earliest bridge players received their groundwork from whist, which is just what you are doing. And they developed into some of the finest card-players the game of bridge has ever known!

In the game that preceded whist, all the suits were treated as equals. Then the concept of a *trump suit* was introduced, contributing to the excitement that swept whist to huge popularity. The great power of the trump suit is that the deuce of trumps can win a trick away from the highest card of a non-trump suit.

However, you cannot play a trump any time you feel like winning a trick. The rule that a player *must* follow suit if possible always applies. But if you have no card of the suit that is led, you *may* play a trump on the trick. If it is the only trump played to that trick, the trick belongs to your side. If more than one trump is played on a trick, the highest trump wins. (The rank of the cards in the trump suit remains unchanged.) A player who has won the previous trick may lead a trump, in which case all must follow suit (if possible) and the highest trump prevails.

For example, suppose diamonds are trumps:

South wins the trick for his side. Since he had no clubs he was free to play a trump, and he played no higher trump than necessary. Naturally, if partner had already played the highest club on the trick, South wouldn't have needed to trump at all.

Thus far the basic principles of play are straightforward. You have learned something about how tricks are won. Now we begin to see why it is valuable for you to be able to name your longest suit as trumps.

Naming the trump suit

How does one name trump? In whist, trump was determined by turning up dealer's last card *or* sometimes, by prior agreement of all four players, that one suit, most often hearts, was always the trump.

If you have lots of high cards in the suits other than trumps, you lead a trump in order to exhaust them before an opponent can trump away your high cards. For example, your hand is:

♠ A K J   ♡ 5 4 3   ◇ A Q J   ♣ K Q J 10.

If you were on lead you would play a heart as often as you

won a trick in order to protect your high cards in the *side* (non-trump) suits.

Suppose you are dealt the following hand:

♠ 10 8 7 5 4 2 ♡ A ◇ K Q J ♣ A K 2.

Your long suit is weak and the short suits are strong.

What are the trick-taking virtues of this hand? Without a trump suit we should expect to win one trick with the ♡A, two tricks with the ♣A and ♣K, and two of our three diamond honors, assuming one of them must lose to the ace. That's a total of five tricks, above the average (3¼, or 13 tricks divided by 4 players). Notice that we weren't able to count any spade winners because we were lacking the top honors. It seems a shame to waste such a long suit.

You could greatly increase the trick-winning value of this hand if you could name spades as trumps. How many tricks is our example hand worth if spades are trumps? (Repeated for convenience: ♠ 10 8 7 5 4 2 ♡ A ◇ K Q J ♣ A K 2.) The honor card tricks in the other suits are still likely to be worth the same five tricks. Why "likely" rather than certain? Because there is a trump suit, and it is possible that an opponent will have been dealt fewer than three diamonds. In that case he may play a trump on one of our diamond honors and so deprive us of the trick (the power of trumps).

To more than compensate for that slight risk, consider what will happen the second time a heart is led. If spades are trumps, you will be able to play the deuce of spades and win the trick for your side. The same thing applies to the fourth *round* of clubs and, in general, subsequent rounds of any of our short suits. We will be taking tricks with our low spades, raising the trick-taking potential of our hand to approximately eight if spades are trumps. Thus, we see that this is a good hand (5 tricks) with no trump suit (or if another suit is trump) but a *very* good hand (8 tricks) if spades are trumps.

So when we come to the bidding by which the right to name the trump suit will be decided (Lesson 5), you can understand why you can bid much more for the right to name spades as trumps. Meanwhile, however, notice that while it would be nice if you had some high cards in the spade suit so you could be sure to remove the opponents' trumps more quickly, the length of your trump suit is of overriding importance.

Let's look at a different type of hand:

♠ 9 ♡ 8 7 ◊ A Q J 7 3 ♣ A K 10 4 2.

Estimating the trick-taking potential of this hand, with hearts or spades as trumps, you expect to win perhaps two of your three diamond honors, plus the two top clubs. However, if diamonds or clubs were named as trumps you could expect to win additional tricks with the low cards in the trump suit, using them to win the second round of spades, the third round of hearts, and of course subsequent rounds of your short suits. Clearly, your hand is more valuable with a trump suit – the question is, which suit?

The diamonds and clubs are equally long and almost equally strong. From your point of view you have no definite preference. You would like to make the choice based on how many cards your partner has in these suits. It would be nice if you could always see his hand before you named the suit – and if you are playing a few practice hands with all of the cards on the table you can do just that. Later, in a real game, when you cannot see your partner's hand, you will have to tell him about the relative length of your suits in the bidding and let him decide which suit he prefers.

For the time being, however, let him put his hand down on the table and let him also see yours. Then you can decide which is your best combined trump suit. Maybe you will discover that he has plenty of high cards in the major suits (spades and hearts) and that the best contract for your combined hands will be no trump suit.

Consider one more hand:

♠ Q 7 5 ♡ Q 10 8 4 ◊ A J 2 ♣ Q J 3

This hand has a different pattern from the others; none of the suits is long or short, the honor cards are fairly evenly distributed. It is very difficult to estimate accurately the number of tricks this hand is worth with nothing as trumps. A rough guess is one trick in each suit – the spades might produce none while hearts or diamonds might produce two. Is there an advantage to naming one suit, say hearts, as trumps? The answer is, not really. First of all, your "long" suit is as short as can be. The most even distribution is our example hand, 13 cards divided among four suits, or three cards per suit with one left over. So, every bridge hand must contain at least one suit that is four cards or longer, which makes the heart suit in our sample hand minimum length for a long suit. How can you, then, name a sensible trump suit?

Trump suit or notrump?

First, you should consult with partner. If he has a long suit you will be happy to abide by his preference. Remember that your objective is to name your best *combined suit* as trumps. If he also holds an evenly distributed hand, you should play this deal without a trump suit. This is called *notrump*. In notrump all suits have equal significance. If a player cannot follow suit he cannot win the trick, as you learned in Lesson 1.

Let's summarize the hands that are worth more tricks played with a trump suit than when played at notrump.

1] Hands of fairly uneven distribution, meaning they contain very short suits (zero, one, or two-card length).

2] Hands with one or more fairly long suits (5 cards or more). With more than one long suit consult partner for a preference. (See bidding). Play in the best combined suit.

Hands that are evenly distributed with neither unusual length nor shortness (*balanced hands*) frequently play best in notrump, assuming partner has no overriding preference.

Quiz No. 2

1] Spades are trumps. West leads the ◇ J, North follows with the ◇ Q, East plays the ♠ 5, and South plays the ♠ 8. Who wins this trick?

2] At notrump North leads the ♣ Q, East follows with the ♣ 5, South plays the ♠ 7, and West the ♣ 9. Who wins the trick?

3] You are on lead with this hand:

♠ A 6 ♡ Q J 10 9 ◇ K Q 3 2 ♣ 9 8 7. Estimate the number of tricks your hand is worth at notrump.

4] Your hand: ♠ 4 ♡ K Q 6 ◇ K J 10 9 8 7 5 ♣ Q 3.
Estimate the number of tricks your hand is worth with diamonds as trumps.

5] With each of the following hands, is it worth more tricks at notrump or with a trump suit? Why?
♠ K 10 9 8 6 ♡ A ◇ Q 8 6 4 2 ♣ 8 4.

6] ♠ K 8 6 ♡ Q 10 3 ◇ J 10 9 2 ♣ A Q 7.

7] ♠ J 4 ♡ A K J 8 6 3 ◇ K J 8 ♣ 10 9.

8] ♠ K 5 ♡ A 8 7 3 ◇ K J 8 2 ♣ A 4 3.

9] What is the name of the process whereby you consult with partner to decide on a trump suit?

Answers to Quiz No. 2

1] **South.** If more than one trump is played on a trick, the highest ranking trump card wins.

2] **North.** Only those who follow suit at notrump are eligible to win the trick.

3] **Four.** One trick in spades, two tricks in hearts (after dislodging the Ace and King), one in diamonds (after driving out the Ace), and none in clubs. These estimates assume no help from partner. If he happens to hold, say, the ♡ K, our heart holding will produce three tricks.

4] **Six.** None in spades, one in hearts, five of your seven diamonds, losing only to the Ace and Queen, and none in clubs. This is a good hand provided diamonds are trumps.

5] **Worth more** with a trump suit (either spades or diamonds). The low cards in our trump suit will produce tricks by trumping hearts and clubs (our short suits).

6] **Worth more** at notrump. The hand is evenly distributed, or balanced. These are typical notrump hands.

7] **Worth more** with hearts as trumps. What is a defect for notrump (short suits) is an asset for suit play.

8] **Worth more** at notrump. This still qualifies as a balanced hand, primarily because there is no long suit.

9] **Bidding.** We begin to discuss this broad subject in Lesson 5.

Lesson 3: starting to play

NOW THAT YOU SEE how tricks are won, you are ready to get the feel of playing bridge. It is unlikely you have three other people reading this book along with you, so let's continue to play alone, with the cards face up.

Playing with trumps

Lay out the cards to help you answer the questions that follow, or play them from the diagrams.

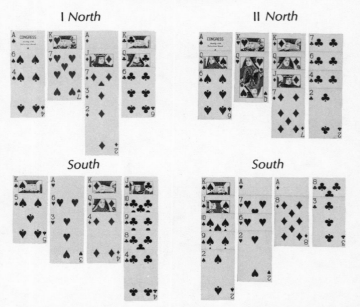

I *North*

II *North*

South

South

In bridge books and magazines (and in the rest of this book), these layouts would be shown as follows:

I *North*
♠ A 6 4
♡ K 7
♢ A J 7 3 2
♣ K Q 6

South
♠ K 5
♡ A 6 3
♢ K Q 4
♣ J 10 9 8 4

II *North*
♠ A Q 6
♡ K Q
♢ K Q J 7
♣ 7 6 4 2

South
♠ K J 10 9 2
♡ A 7 6 2
♢ A 8
♣ 8 3

Consider these hands separately. Imagine that you are South and you are looking at the cards your partner (North) is holding. In Example I, try to calculate how many tricks you would win if:

a] clubs were trumps;
b] diamonds were trumps;
c] you were playing at notrump.

Attempt these problems before reading further.

Let us tackle one problem at a time, starting

with (a) where clubs are trumps. Holding eight trumps in the combined hands, generally the minimum number required for a good trump suit, it can be seen that you will win four of the five clubs in the South hand, losing only to the Ace. Your plan is to play a low club towards North's King. After you have forced out the Ace, your side owns all the high cards in the suit. The opponents may take the Ace now or later, but it is the only trick they will win in the suit. You will play clubs until neither opponent has any more low trumps.

In the diamond suit you expect to win five tricks. Since your side has eight cards in diamonds, the opponents have the remaining five. If those five enemy cards are divided 3–2 or 4–1 between their two hands, you will extract them all by playing the King and Queen from your hand (North following with the two and three) and then continuing with North's Ace-Jack. This should eliminate all the diamonds from the opposing hands, which makes North's last diamond a long card winner. Only if one opponent holds all five outstanding diamonds (very unlikely) will North's fifth diamond not be good for a trick. In hearts and spades you can win two tricks in each suit by virtue of owning the two highest honor cards, which of course you will use to win separate tricks.

Thus, you will lose only one trick (to the Ace of clubs) and win the remaining twelve, an excellent result.

Situation (b), where diamonds are trumps, yields exactly the same result, twelve tricks. The only difference in the sequence of plays is that you would play diamonds first to take out the opposing trumps. Otherwise, you run the risk of allowing an opponent to trump away one of your winning tricks. Remember that the two of trumps beats the Ace of any other suit, so in general it is good practice to draw the enemy trumps very early in the hand.

Situation (c) at notrump provides the same twelve tricks! Here the suit you should play first is clubs, because that is where the greatest number of tricks can be *established*. Establishment is an important concept of play. Note that in spades, hearts, and diamonds your winning tricks are just waiting to be taken. In clubs, though, you have no immediate tricks; winners need to be established by driving out the opponents' Ace. Once the Ace is gone you have four winners to add to your immediate winners.

In Example II, try the same type of calculation, assuming: (*a*) spades are trumps, and (*b*) you are playing at notrump. Again, for your own benefit, read no further until you have worked each problem.

Beginning with (*a*) where spades are trumps, South can expect to win all five spades in his hand since his side owns all the high cards in that suit; three heart tricks–North's King-Queen plus South's Ace, provided that South underplays North's winners with low hearts; the four top diamond honors in the combined hands, again provided that South does not play two of his winners on the same trick (North should play the ♢ 7 under South's Ace), and no club trick. This seems to give South 12 winners, but this is not necessarily the case.

When you are *declaring* a bridge hand – in these examples South is the declarer and North, his partner, is the *dummy* – the *defenders* have the right to make the first or *opening lead*. Specifically, the player to the left of the declarer plays first, and suppose he chooses to lead a club in our Example II. Since the defenders own all the high clubs, they will have no difficulty in winning the first and second round of the suit. If they play clubs a third time, South can trump with a high spade in his hand and then proceed to draw the opposing trumps and win the rest of the tricks, but his total will be eleven winners, not twelve – thirteen total tricks, minus two losers = eleven tricks. Of course, the opening lead by the defense might not be a club, in which case declarer will not lose his two low clubs. This illustrates the power of the opening lead, a factor that will often influence whether declarer wishes to play in a trump suit or at notrump, as witness situation (*b*) in Example II.

Playing at notrump South can produce twelve winners (five spades, three hearts, and four diamonds) as soon as he gains the lead. Unfortunately for declarer, West (his left-hand opponent) is on lead, and if the defenders start clubs they will win as many tricks as they have long cards in that suit. With seven clubs missing, the most favorable division declarer can hope for is 4–3, so that he loses only four tricks. If the clubs are more unevenly divided, he will lose more than four tricks, as he helplessly discards winners. Therefore, notrump is much inferior to spades in this example. An unguarded suit is usually a fatal flaw at notrump; that is the most important lesson of this hand.

These two examples point out the value of the right to name the declaration, whether it be a suit or notrump. This final declaration is said to be the *contract,* hence the term contract bridge. The declarer's side contracts to win a certain minimum number of tricks in the trump suit (or notrump) of its choice. To gain this privilege they must outbid their opponents, who are also aware of the advantages in naming the final declaration. The *bidding* naturally precedes the play, and it is to this crucial area that we will now turn our attention.

In Examples I and II, you were trying to decide the best final contract, looking at both your hand and your partner's. But in a real bridge game you will not be able to see partner's cards while in the process of deciding the best contract, nor will he see yours. You and partner will be describing your hand through bids, while the opponents do the same. The object of bidding is communication; it is a type of language. You try to describe your hand values, and to do so you have to measure these values. The way hand values have been measured for many years now is the Goren Point Count. It is widely accepted and easy to learn.

Point count

Point Count assigns the following numerical values to honor cards:

Ace = **4** *Points;* King = **3** *Points;* Queen = **2** *Points;* Jack = **1** *Point.*

The entire deck contains 40 *High Card* Points (HCP), making the average share for each hand 10 HCP.

In addition to High Card Points a player should count *Short Suit* Points as an asset, since we have seen how, at a trump contract, being short in a suit limits the number of tricks the opponents can win in it. Short suit points are computed by counting 1 point for only two cards in any suit; 2 points for only one card in a suit; and 3 points for no card in any suit. The total worth of a hand combines High Card Points plus short suit points.

Let's compute the value of a few hands for practice. Suppose you hold ♠ A Q 7 6 ♡ K J 8 ◇ 10 9 ♣ Q J 7 2. This hand is worth a total of 15 points, broken down as follows:

♠ A Q 7 6	- **6**	High Card Points
♡ K J -	**4** HCP + **1** SSP	
◇ 10 9 -	**0** HCP + **1** SSP	
♣ Q J 7 2 -	**3** HCP	
	15 Total Points	

Evaluate this hand:

♠ K J 8 6 3 ♡ A ◇ Q 10 9 7 4 2 ♣ 9.

The **HCP** amount to 10, 4 in ♠, 4 in ♡, and 2 in ◇, an average high card hand. What makes this hand better than average, though, are the two long suits with their potential for extra tricks. The short suit points add to 4, 2 for each suit with only one card. This brings the total worth of this hand to 14 points, 10 **HCP** plus 4 **SSP**. Even at this early stage, you can see that the Point Count is a sensible sliding scale that reflects a hand's trick-taking potential.

Soon you will learn what bids to make, based on your hand's

evaluation. Certain bids show a specific amount of points. Some also describe your *distribution* – the pattern of your hand: which suits are long, which are short. As the bidding progresses, each player can develop a picture of what his partner's hand looks like, and it is on this basis that they will decide on their best final contract. Naturally, it would be easier if you could just peek at your partner's hand, as we did at the beginning of this chapter. But this is not only illegal, it would make the game of bridge much less the beautiful challenge that it is.

In the next chapter we will study the scoring table to see how it affects the bidding. You will learn that there are bonuses to reward you for bidding as much as you can make, but you can already see a reward for outbidding the opponents. It gives you the advantage of naming the trump suit or whether the hand will play at notrump. This lets you win as many tricks as possible on each hand, which is, after all, the object of the game.

Quiz No. 3

In questions 1–6, look at the pair of hands and decide at which contract (specific suit or notrump) you could win the most tricks.

1] ♠ Q J 6
    ♡ K J 8 6
    ◇ A Q 5
    ♣ K 9 8

    ♠ K 7 5 3
    ♡ Q 5 4
    ◇ K 3
    ♣ Q J 6 3

2] ♠ 10 9 8
    ♡ A J 8 6 4 2
    ◇ K 8
    ♣ K 5

    ♠ Q J 7 6 2
    ♡ 7
    ◇ Q 5
    ♣ A 7 6 3 2

3] ♠ A 8 7 6
    ♡ J 10 3
    ◇ A K 9 6 2
    ♣ 7 `

    ♠ K 4 3 2
    ♡ 7 6
    ◇ 10 8
    ♣ A K 6 5 4

4] ♠ Q 5 4 2
    ♡ J 8 7 3
    ◇ 6 4 2
    ♣ 9 8

    ♠ 9 8 7 6
    ♡ 8 6
    ◇ J 9 8
    ♣ J 10 8 7

5] ♠ K 7 4
    ♡ A
    ◇ Q 6 5 3 2
    ♣ K Q J 7

    ♠ Q
    ♡ 9 7 6
    ◇ J 10 9 7 4
    ♣ A 10 9 8

6] ♠ A 6 4 2
    ♡ K Q J
    ◇ A 7 3
    ♣ 7 6 5

    ♠ 9 8
    ♡ 7 2
    ◇ 10 9 8 4 2
    ♣ A K J 2

1

2

3

4

5

6

In questions 7–10 evaluate the total point value of each hand – high card points plus short-suit points.

7] ♠ A J 7 ♡ K Q 5 2 ◊ J 8 6 4 ♣ 10 9
8] ♠ K Q 6 5 3 ♡ 9 ◊ A 4 ♣ Q J 8 7 2
9] ♠ 9 7 ♡ Q J 6 ◊ A J 8 6 4 2 ♣ 8 3
10] ♠ K Q J 7 ♡ A Q J 6 2 ◊ 7 ♣ A K J

Answers to Quiz No. 3

1] **Notrump.** The hands lack a combined eight card trump suit, and each suit is well guarded.

2] **Spades.** Even though hearts is the longest suit held by one player, spades is the longest combined suit that should generally be chosen as trumps.

3] **Spades.** There is only one eight-card (combined) suit. Lack of a guard in hearts makes notrump a poor contract.

4] **You should expect the opponents to play this contract.** They have by far the stronger hands, which means they will outbid you and win the declaration.

5] **Diamonds.** The clubs are stronger but the diamonds are longer, and when they are not equal, length is more important for a trump suit than strength.

6] **Diamonds.** Notrump is the second best contract, because if the opponents lead spades they will drive out your only guard in the suit, leaving you wide open when you next lose the lead. In a diamond contract, though, they can only win one spade trick (at most) because the third round of the suit can be trumped.

7] **12 points,** 11 in high cards: 5 in spades, 5 in hearts, and 1 in diamonds. 1 short suit point in clubs.

8] **15 points.** 12 HCP plus 1 point for the two diamonds and 2 for the one heart.

9] **10 points.** 8 HCP plus 2 short suit points, 1 for each two-card suit.

10] **23 points.** 6 HCP in spades, 7 HCP in hearts, 4 HCP in diamonds, and 4 HCP in clubs, plus 2 short suit points for the lone diamond. A marvelous hand!

Lesson 4: scoring

Here are some examples of how tricks are won:

At the left is a sample of a rubber bridge scoresheet. "We" means your partnership; "they" means the opponents. The heavy line across the center separates points scored towards *game*, which go *below the line,* and overtricks, penalty points, and bonuses which are written above the line.

The first pair to score two games wins the *rubber.* Game equals 100 points (or more) below the line. Game can be scored in one deal by bidding and making 5 ♣ or 5 ◊, 4 ♡ or 4 ♠, or 3NT(notrump). These totals are based on the value of tricks in the different denominations: ♣ and ◊ (the *minor* suits) = 20 points per trick; ♡ and ♠ (the *major* suits) = 30 points per trick; NT=40 for the first trick and 30 for each subsequent trick, or 40+30+30.

Game can also be scored by combining two (or more) *part scores (partials)* that total at least 100 points. For instance, bidding and making a contract of 2 ♠ (30+30=60) followed by bidding and making 1NT (40) produce a game, provided the opponents have not scored a game in the meantime. When one side scores a game, a line is drawn across the score. All previous part scores no longer count as a step toward the next game.

One other way to score a game is to play and make a doubled contract. The call of *double* has the effect of doubling the points that would ordinarily be scored below the line: 2 ♡ = 60 (30+30); 2 ♡ doubled=120 (60 × 2), or game. In addition, there is a 50 point bonus (entered above the line) for making any doubled contract.

Bonuses for bidding and making a *slam*: Bidding and making a bid of six (twelve tricks) is called a *small slam*. A contract to win all thirteen tricks is a *grand slam*. Since these are the hardest contracts to make, they are rewarded with large bonuses.

What happens when you fail to make what you bid? The opponents score a *penalty* above the line. The size of the penalty depends on whether you are *vulnerable*. (Vulnerable means you have already scored one game towards the rubber.) Vulnerable penalties are 100 points per undertrick; non-vulnerable (when your side has not yet scored a game) penalties are 50 points for each trick by which you fall short. If the final contract is doubled the penalties are increased. (*See chart below*.) Remember, all penalty points are scored above the line.

Finally, if the final contract is *redoubled,* the score is twice that of a doubled contract, whether it makes or fails.

Bonuses (above the line) are scored as follows:

Winning the rubber: 700 if won two games to none; 500 if won two games to one.

Bidding and making a small slam: 500 not vulnerable, 750 vulnerable.

Bidding and making a grand slam: 1000 not vulnerable, 1500 vulnerable.

An *unfinished rubber* (whatever the reason) carries a bonus of 300 for a side that is one game ahead. A part score in an unfinished game counts 50.

Honors: If any player holds in his own hand five honors (A K Q J 10) in the trump suit, or all four aces at notrump,

150 points. For four of the five honors in the trump suit, 100 points.

Penalty points for doubled contracts

	Not Vulnerable	Vulnerable
Down One	100	200
Down Two	300	500
Each additional undertrick	200	300

If declarer makes a contract that has been doubled, he scores double the trick score below the line plus a 50 point bonus, as already mentioned. If declarer makes his doubled contract with overtricks, each overtrick is worth 100 when not vulnerable; 200 when vulnerable. Remember, a redouble doubles all these awards, except the 50 point bonus for making contract. This scoring method, devised in 1925 by the father of contract bridge, Harold Vanderbilt, is the heart of the game. The quiz which follows will help make it clear to you. The same scoring situations constantly recur; practice will make scoring automatic. And since many scorepads are accompanied by a scoring table, there is no need to memorize.

Quiz No. 4

1] Which of these contracts, if made, equals game? 2NT, 4 ♠, 4 ♣, 5 ♢?

2] Which of these contracts is a slam? 5 ♣, 4NT, 6 ♡, 7 ♠?

3] How many points do you score for bidding 3NT and making 4?

4] How many points do you score for bidding 3 ♣ and making 5?

5] What is it worth to you if the opponents bid 4 ♡ and fail by two tricks, vulnerable?

6] The opponents overbid to 3 ◇, doubled and set two, not vulnerable. Your score?

7] You bid and make 6 ◇, not vulnerable. What is your score, both above and below the line?

8] Your partner plays 4 ♡ and is set (goes down) one, redoubled and vulnerable. How much does this cost you?

9] You bid and make 4 ♠ not vulnerable, holding the A K Q 10 of spades. What is your total score?

10] Twice in succession your side bids 4 ♡ making 5. What is your total score for the rubber?

Answers to Quiz No. **4**

1] **4 ♠** (30 × 4) and 5 ◇ (20 × 5).

2] **6 ♡** (small slam) and 7 ♠ (grand slam).

3] **130.** 100 (40+30+30) below the line, and 30 (overtrick) above.

4] **60** (20 × 3) below the line, and 40 (20 × 2) above. This is a partial; remember, you must *bid* game to receive credit for it.

5] **200** (100 per undertrick).

6] **300.** (Consult chart.)

7] **620.** 120 (20 × 6) below the line, and 500 small slam bonus above. And you now have all the extra risks and gains of being vulnerable.

8] **400.** Down one doubled and vulnerable is 200; a redouble multiplies the score by 2.

9] **220.** 120 (30 × 4) below the line, and 100 above for the honors. This first game makes you vulnerable.

10] **1000.** This is computed as follows: 240 for game contracts (below), 60 for overtricks (above), and 700 rubber bonus— two games to none (above). Congratulations on your victory!

Here is the score of a typical rubber

WE	THEY
	200(e)
	150 (d)
500(f)	50 (b)
750 (f)	60 (a)
100 (c)	60 (a)
	120(d)
180(f)	
Total score:	
1530	640

(a) The opponents bid 2 ♠ and made four. They scored 60 for tricks bid for (below the line) and another 60 above for overtricks.

(b) They set you one trick, not doubled at 3 ♡ but they could have made 2 ♠, which they had bid, giving them the first game (60 added to the 60 they already have) so you have actually gained. Even if they had doubled you, the penalty would have been only 100, but you would still have had a good result, losing only 40 points and keeping them from making game.

(c) You bid and made 3 NT. You have scored the first game, and a line is drawn below the score thus far. Their 60 will no longer count toward winning the next game, although it is scored at the end when you total the rubber. You are now vulnerable.

(d) They bid and made 4 ♠, receiving 120 below and 150 above for five honors in one hand. Each side now has a game and is vulnerable. The winner of the next game will win the rubber.

(e) You bid 5 ◇ to prevent the opponents from making the rubber for having bid 4 ♠, which they could have made. They double and set you one trick, scoring 200 above the line. This was a good sacrifice for you, since they would have scored 620 points for making 4 ♠ and the rubber: 120 below; 500 above.

(f) You bid and make 6 ♡, scoring 180 below (30 × 6), and two bonuses above: 500 for winning the rubber; 750 for making the slam.

Can you figure out what the difference in the rubber score

would have been if they had bid and made 4 ♠ on hand (a), instead of bidding only 2 ♠?

They would have won the rubber, scoring their second game on hand (d). Their score would have been 940, since they would receive the 500 point bonus and the rubber would have ended after hand (d), so you would have scored only 100 points and they would have won 840. But, much more important, you would not have had the chance to bid and make your small slam on hand (f) because the rubber would have been over. Instead of your winning 890, you would have lost 840 and the total difference in the result would have been 1730 points.

Here, by observing the effect of the scoring table, you are beginning to get an idea of why it is important to bid a game if you have a good chance to make it. Risking being set 50 points (or 100 if you doubled) on the first hand, supposing they had been able to make only 3 ♠, would have been a very favorable proposition.

Also, by saving the rubber at a cost of 200 points on hand (e), you showed a tremendous profit.

Knowing the scoring will help you judge what you should bid in order to be able to name the contract and outbid the opponents. You will learn how to judge this better when you have read the next chapters.

Lesson 5: valuing your hand for bidding

You have seen how tricks are won: by *high cards;* by *long cards* which become winners after the high cards in that suit have been played; and by *trumping,* when you no longer have a card of the suit that is led.

Up to now, you have been able to select what you think may be best for your side by actually seeing and comparing your hand with partner's. But in a real game, you will not be able to see your partner's hand. You can tell each other your high cards and your suit lengths only by *bidding.*

Bidding is a kind of code that includes only fifteen words: the *levels,* from one to seven; the *names of the four suits,* spades, hearts, diamonds and clubs; *notrump,* which means a willingness to play without a trump suit; *pass* (which means that you make no bid; in fact, in England the term for pass was once "no bid" and in many games this is still used); and the words *double* and *redouble,* which nominally mean that you wish to increase the penalties you collect if you set the opponents (double), or that you expect to make the contract which has been doubled and would like to collect more for that accomplishment (re-double).

The dealer has the first turn to bid or pass. The player to his left is next to speak. The turn to bid passes clockwise around the table. If all four players elect to pass, there is a new deal by the player at the previous dealer's left.

If any player makes a *bid,* each player in turn may make a

higher bid. The bidding ends when the last bid is followed by three passes. The last bid preceding three passes becomes the *contract* – the declaration, either a suit or notrump and the number of tricks which the bid contracts to take over and above six. The first six tricks won are called "the book." The seventh trick is the odd trick. A bid of one undertakes to win seven tricks; a two bid undertakes to win eight, etc.

The rank of the bids

You cannot name a bid unless it is higher than the preceding bid. A bid may be higher because it is for the same number of tricks in a higher ranking suit, or for a greater number of tricks.

The suits rank clubs (♣) lowest, diamonds (◇), hearts (♡) and spades (♠) highest. A bid in notrump ranks higher than the bid of any suit. If the preceding bid is 1 ♡, it can be overbid at the one level only by 1 ♠ or 1 NT. If you wish to bid clubs or diamonds over 1 ♡, you must bid at a higher level – at least 2 ♣ or 2 ◇. Any bid of two ranks higher than any bid of one; a bid of three overbids any bid of two, etc. An insufficient bid – one which does not rank higher than the preceding bid – is cancelled and the side that makes it may be subject to a penalty.

Your first bid

Your first bid of one in a suit tells partner that you have more than your average share of high cards and at least four cards* in the suit you bid. A major suit of only four cards must include two of the four top honors to be biddable. The minimum holding would be Q J 9 2. For a minor suit opening, this high-card requirement can be relaxed. But any five card or longer suit is biddable.

When you open the bidding, therefore, you are telling partner

*In certain cases, as you will learn later, you may have only three clubs or three diamonds.

about the two most important trick-winning features of your hand: your high cards and your suit length. If you pass, you announce that you do not have sufficient strength to promise partner that you expect to win at least four or five tricks, of which at least two-plus must be high card tricks which you expect will win the first or second lead of a suit. These tricks are called defensive tricks, because partner can rely on them no matter what the final contract may be.

Compare these hands:

a]	♠ A 10 9 3 2	b]	♠ Q J 10 9 8 7
	♡ A 4 3		♡ A 4
	◇ A 4		◇ 10 2
	♣ Q 9 7		♣ Q J 10

Hand a) is likely to win five tricks with spades as trumps. Assuming that the remaining eight spades are favorably divided, you will win two long card tricks – or perhaps one long card trick and one trick by ruffing a third round of diamonds – in addition to your three aces.

Hand b) will probably win six tricks: the ♡ A and, after the ♠ A and ♠ K and ♣ A and ♣ K are out, four spade tricks and one club trick. So hand b) is potentially worth one more trick than hand a).

Nevertheless, you may open the bidding with 1 ♠ on a), but you should not open with 1 ♠ on b). Why? Because you would be promising two high card tricks and you do not have them. Given the opportunity, you will bid spades later. Once you have passed, your partner will no longer count on you for two defensive high card tricks.

How to value your hand

You do not always have your high card tricks in Aces and King-Queens in the same suit. In order to value your high cards, you use a point count that gives each high card a point value:

Ace = 4 points
King = 3 points
Queen = 2 points
Jack = 1 point

Since there are 40 high card points in the pack, an average hand will hold 10 points in high cards. If you have 13 high card points (HCP) you should try to open the bidding. However, you might pass, for example, with:

♠ A 5 4
♡ K 9 4 3
♦ Q J 7
♣ K 7 6

You have 13 HCP, but you have no distributional points and your trick-winning potential is limited. However, with:

♠ A 5 4
♡ K 9 4
♦ Q 8 7
♣ K Q 9 6

you will bid. You have 14 HCP and a four-card suit (clubs) headed by two high honors.

Measuring distributional values

As you know, there are two ways to win tricks other than by high cards: by long cards which will win tricks when the higher cards of the suit have been played, and by trumping when you no longer have a card of the suit that is led. Until I introduced a method of valuing these *distributional* features in the same kind of points by which you measure high cards, it was difficult to combine these different kind of values. Now, however, you can measure them this way:

Doubleton (only two cards in a suit) – 1 point
Singleton (only one card in a suit) – 2 points
Void (no card in a suit) – 3 points.

You may count more than one of these values whenever they are present.

These distributional points roughly measure both your ruffing values and your long card values. Add your high card points to your distributional points. If you have 13 points, look for a bid. If you have 14 points, of which at least 10 are HCP, you should open the bidding.

Going back to hands a) and b) at the beginning of this lesson, let us measure your trick-winning values in points.

		HCP	Dist.			HCP	Dist.
a]	♠ A 10 9 3 2	4		b]	♠ Q J 10 9 8 7	3	
	♡ A 4 3	4			♡ A 4	4	1
	◇ A 4	4	1		◇ 10 2		1
	♣ Q 9 7	2			♣ Q J 10	3	
	Total	**14 plus 1**				**10 plus 2**	

You bid 1 ♠ on hand a) because you have a total of 15 points. You pass hand b) because you have only 12 points, including distribution.

Be wary of opening the bidding unless you have two winning high card tricks at any contract.

The plus value of aces

On borderline openings, if a 13-point hand does not include an Ace, pass. Aces have an extra value. While they do not take more than one trick, they can win the *first* trick in a suit, and thus prevent the opponents from winning tricks immediately. As a measure of this extra value:

Add one point if your hand contains all four Aces.

Thus, if you hold all four Aces you can count them as 17 points instead of 16.

Valuing unbalanced hands

A hand that includes a singleton or a void is said to be *unbalanced*. The more unbalanced it is, the more it is likely to be worth because of distributional points. Here is a hand similar to some you encountered in the earlier lessons:

	HCP	Dist.
♠ A Q 8 7 4	6	
♡ K J 10 9 2	4	
◇ 9	–	2
♣ K 5	3	1
Total	**13**	**3**

On high card points alone, this hand is easily worth an opening bid. But when you add the distributional points, the total is 16. Therefore, it is worth bidding twice. If partner has no support for one suit, he may have good support for the second. In any case, this hand will usually be more valuable at suit play than at notrump because of your ability to limit the losers in your short suits by trumping, and your ability to establish your second long suit under the protection of your partnership's better combined trump suit.

Valuing balanced hands

Most of the values of balanced hands will come from high cards. When you have sufficient high cards to equal the combined value of the unbalanced hand we have just examined–16 HCP–you may open the bidding with 1 NT. This shows a hand worth 16 to 18 points, all in high cards. For example.

		HCP			HCP			HCP
a]	♠ K Q 4	5	b]	♠ K Q 4 2	5	c]	♠ K Q 4 2	5
	♡ Q J 2	3		♡ K 2	3		♡ Q 2	2
	◇ A 6 5	4		◇ A 6 5	4		◇ A 6 5	4
	♣ K J 9 4	4_		♣ K J 9 4	4_		♣ K J 9 4	4_
		16			16			15

You open hands a) and b) with 1 NT because they total 16 HCP. (It is OK to open 1 NT with a doubleton, even if it contains no sure trick – but not with more than one doubleton.) However, you cannot open hand c) with 1 NT because it counts only 15 points. True, if you added 1 point for the doubleton heart, it would come to 16, but distributional points do not count in NT evaluation. Of course, hand c) easily qualifies for a bid of 1 in a suit.

Here is a quiz reviewing what you have learned in this lesson.

Quiz No. 5

1] Arrange these denominations in their correct order of rank from highest to lowest: ◇, ♠, NT, ♣, ♡.

2] Which of these would not be a legal bidding sequence? Why?

   a] 1 ♡ Pass 1 NT 2 ♣

   b] 1 ♡ Pass 2 ♣ 1 NT

   c] 1 ♣ Pass 1 NT 2 ♣

3] What marks the official end of an auction?

4] How many points do you need as a minimum to open with a bid of one in a suit? How many in high cards alone?

5] How many points do you need to open with 1 NT? How many in high cards?

6] Which of these hands fails to qualify for an opening bid of 1 NT? Why?

a] ♠ K Q 8   b] ♠ A 8 7 6   c] ♠ K 10 5 3
    ♡ K Q 8   ♡ 10 2   ♡ A
    ◇ K Q 4 2   ◇ K Q J 2   ◇ A Q 5 3
    ♣ A 6 2   ♣ A Q J 3   ♣ K 9 5 3

7]   Which of these hands qualifies as an opening bid of one in a suit? Why?

a] ♠ 9 8 6 4 3   b] ♠ A 4 2   c] ♠ J 2
    ♡ A J   ♡ K 7 6   ♡ K Q J 9 2
    ◇ K Q 2   ◇ Q 7 5 3   ◇ Q J 5
    ♣ K 9 6   ♣ K 9 8   ♣ Q 10 8

8]   What happens when all four players pass on the first round of bidding?

Answers to Quiz No. 5

1]   **NT, ♠, ♡, ◇, ♣.**

2]   b) **1 NT is not sufficient to bid over 2 ♣.** A bid must be higher in rank or at a higher level. c) is tricky, but correct. There is nothing to prevent a player from bidding the same suit as his opponents have already bid, as long as his bid is sufficient to overcall the last bid.

3]   **Three passes** following a bid.

4]   **13.** 10 in HCP.

5]   **16 HCP.** All points must be in high cards for NT bidding.

6]   **a) because it counts 19 HCP**, too many for a 1 NT bid. **c) because it includes a singleton** and is therefore not a balanced hand. It does not matter that the singleton is the Ace.

7]   **Only a)** is a sound opening bid of 1 ♠; remember, any five-card or longer suit is biddable. Hand b) has only 12 points and no distributional values; and c) includes 13 points but does not contain two first- or second-round tricks.

8]   **The cards are thrown in** and a new deal from a shuffled pack is made by the player at the first dealer's left.

Lesson **6**: the bidding begins

We have seen why it is an advantage to be able to select the best place to play the combined hands of you and your partner. It is this advantage that you are bidding for, plus the chance to win one or more of the bonuses listed in the scoring table. If you bid too much, the opponents will score a penalty and you will have lost credit for any lesser bid you might have made. If you bid too little, you will have lost the opportunity to score a game or a slam.

The first bid is the foundation on which the bidding success will be based. Thus, the first information you want to give your partner is whether you have the values for an opening bid (if not, you will pass) and if so, where those values lie – especially the suit or suits in which you have length.

Count your points first

The value of a hand is computed in points that take into account both high cards and distribution. For practice, let's compute the value of a few more hands:

a]		HCP	Dist.	b]		HCP	Dist.
	♠ J 10 8	1			♠ K Q 8 6 3	5	
	♡ K 9	3	1		♡ A	4	2
	◇ Q J 9 2	3			◇ Q J 10 7 4 2	3	
	♣ A Q 7 6	6			♣ 9	0	1
		13	1			12	3

		HCP	Dist.
c]	♠ K Q 6	5	
	♡ K Q J 2	6	
	◇ A 5	4	1
	♣ Q 8 3 2	2	
		17	1

Each of these hands is worth an opening bid. a) because you have 13 HCP plus 1 for the doubleton; b) because you have 12 HCP which include two high card tricks, plus 3 for distribution; c) because you have 17 points in high cards alone. Therefore, you do not pass, which would tell your partner that you hold a weaker hand. The question is, what do you bid?

Hand c) is easy because you have 17 HCP and a balanced distribution. You bid 1 NT. But each of the other two includes two biddable suits.

Which suit to bid first

The answer to a) and b) is 1 ◇. How can you decide? Study the following guideline table:

1] With two five-card or longer suits of equal length, bid the higher-ranking first.

2] With two suits of unequal length, bid the longer suit first.

3] With two four-card biddable suits, open the higher ranking if the suits are adjacent (touching in rank, such as ♠ and ♡; ♡ and ◇, etc.)

4] With two non-adjacent four-card biddable suits, open the suit that ranks directly below your short suit.

5] With three four-card biddable suits, open the suit that ranks directly below the singleton. (i.e., with a singleton heart, bid 1 ◇; with a singleton club, open 1 ♠.)

Thus in the preceding example a), you bid 1 ◇ because it is the higher of touching suits. In example b), you bid 1 ◇ because it is the longer suit. As long as you have the point values for an opening bid, do not let it concern you that the longer suit is not as strong in high cards as the shorter.

Count the point value of these example hands and decide what you would bid.

a] ♠ Q 2   b] ♠ A J 8 6   c] ♠ Q J 8
    ♡ Q 10 6 5 4   ♡ 9 8   ♡ K 4
    ◇ A K J 10   ◇ K Q 7 5   ◇ A 10 9 4
    ♣ K 3   ♣ J 8 7   ♣ A Q 6 5

d] ♠ K Q 10 3   e] ♠ 10   f] ♠ 9
    ♡ A J   ♡ K 7   ♡ A J 8 7
    ◇ A 9 8 7   ◇ K Q 9 7 2   ◇ K 10 9 8
    ♣ 8 7 6   ♣ A K J 8 6   ♣ A Q 4 2

a] Bid 1 ♡. 15 HCP, plus 1 point each for your two doubletons.

b] Pass. You have only 11 HCP, plus 1 for the doubleton.

c] Bid 1 NT. You have 16 HCP with balanced distribution.

d] Bid 1 ◇. 14 HCP plus 1 for the doubleton heart. You choose 1 ◇ because it is just below your doubleton.

e] Bid 1 ◇. 16 HCP plus 3 distributional points. With two five-card suits, open the higher ranking.

f] Bid 1 ♡. 14 HCP plus 2 for the singleton. With three four-card suits, open the suit ranking directly below the singleton.

An exception to the rule.

Sometimes you will pick up a hand like this:

♠ A 8 7 ♡ J 10 6 2 ◇ A Q 5 ♣ Q J 3.

You have 14 HCP – too strong to pass, yet your only four-card suit, hearts, is not biddable. The hand lacks the 16 HCP needed to open 1 NT, so you have met the exception mentioned in Lesson 5. The solution is to bid 1 ♣. The principle is that you bid your lower three-card minor when you don't own any other biddable suit. Don't worry that you have only three cards in your *minor* suit (◇ or ♣). It is more important not to mislead partner by bidding an unbiddable four-card *major* (♠ or ♡) because the majority of game contracts are played in the major suits. Mostly, this is because you need to bid only 4 of the major (10 tricks) to make a game, whereas you need to bid 5 in a minor (11 tricks). Therefore, partner will not be too enthusiastic about raising a minor suit bid (as you will learn in Lesson 7). If he does raise, he will have at least four and more often five or more.

What you need to bid game

When the combined hands of you and your partner uncover a mutually agreeable final contract – a "fit" – as a general rule the minimum number of points you need in the combined hands to bid for game or slam are:

3 NT, 4 ♡ or 4 ♠ – 26 points
5 ♣ or 5 ◊ – 29 points
Small slam (12 tricks) – 33 points
Grand slam (13 tricks) – 37 points

Sometimes you will be able to make these contracts with slightly fewer points; sometimes you will NOT be able to make them with slightly more. Your results will depend on how well your hands fit. But you will be wise to use these figures as a general guide. For example, if your side holds 37 HCP, you cannot be missing an ace. If you have 33, you cannot be missing more than an ace and a king.

Why you open with 13 points

If you hold 13 points and your partner holds 13, you have the necessary total to bid for game, provided you uncover a suitable fit in a major or have the necessary high cards in all four suits to make 3 NT. Therefore, the general guide is:

An opening bid facing an opening bid equals a game.

In bridge, 13 is the magic number. There are 13 cards in a suit, 13 cards in each hand, 13 tricks in each deal. This makes it easy to remember that you need a minimum of 13 points to open.

The reason why your opening bid must include two-plus high-card tricks (A, A–K, K–Q, or the equivalent) is that there are about 8½ high card tricks in every deal. To have hopes of game, you and your partner combined should hold a majority of these quick winners. If you have a bare majority, you must have an excellent fit and shortage in the suits that are weak, otherwise the opponents will be able to take too many tricks against you before you can score the tricks you need for game. In the average deal, eight or nine tricks are won by high cards; the rest are won by long cards or by trumping.

There is another reason for opening the bidding, but a lesser one. If the opponents outbid you, you hope that your first bid will help your partner to find the safest opening lead.

After partner has passed

If your partner has already passed, of course you will want more than 13 points to open the bidding, because you know that your combined hands will not offer much chance to make game. Even a 14-point hand may be passed out when your partner has already passed, especially if it does not include a strong suit.

Maximum strength for bid of 1 in a suit

You have learned that the minimum strength for an opening bid of 1 in a suit is 13. The maximum is 21. (Not all hands between 13 and 21 are opened with 1 in a suit. Balanced hands in the 16–18 point range are opened with 1 NT.) With 26 high card points in the combined hands, you will be aiming at a game bid. The reason for this range of up to 21 will be seen when we come to examine the action by the opener's partner—the *responding* hand.

The quiz for this lesson includes questions composed of two parts: 1) What is the point count of the hand, including points for distribution? 2) What is the correct opening bid?

Quiz No. **6**

1]   ♠ K J 5 4 3   ♡ Q J 8 7   ◇ A K 2   ♣ 10   *1 ♠*

2]   ♠ A Q 5 3   ♡ K Q 6 4   ◇ Q 5 4   ♣ K J   *1 NT*

3] ♠ Q 10 9 ♡ A 3 2 ◇ Q 10 7 6 5 ♣ K 9

4] ♠ Q 5 ♡ Q J 7 5 ◇ A J 8 ♣ A J 6 4

5] ♠ K J 10 9 ♡ A Q J 6 ◇ 7 5 ♣ Q J 9

6] ♠ 8 ♡ A K 8 6 3 ◇ K Q J 10 6 ♣ 9 7

7] ♠ K Q 8 6 ♡ A J 5 2 ◇ K J 10 8 ♣ 7

8] ♠ void ♡ Q J 10 7 ◇ A 10 8 7 5 ♣ K Q J 7

9] ♠ A 8 5 4 ♡ K 9 8 7 ◇ A 10 ♣ K 5 3

10] ♠ A K 8 6 ♡ A Q J 10 4 ◇ K Q ♣ 10 9

Answers to Quiz No. 6

1] 16 points (14 HCP plus 2 for the singleton). Open 1 ♠, your longest suit.

2] 17 points (all HCP). Open 1 NT. This is better than the alternate possibility – 1 ♠ – because it best describes your balanced hand with a single bid. (Later, you will learn how partner can steer the contract into a four-card major if he has one.)

3] 12 points. (11 HCP plus 1 for doubleton club.) Pass. This hand is just under the strength of an opening bid.

4] 16 points. (15 HCP plus 1 for doubleton.) Open 1 ♡. The clubs are also biddable, of course, but since the two suits are not adjacent, it is better to open in the suit below the one in which you are short.

5] 15 points. (14 HCP plus 1 for doubleton diamond.) Bid 1 ♠, the higher of two biddable adjacent suits.

6] 16 points. (13 HCP plus 1 for doubleton club and 2 for singleton spade.) Open 1 ♡. With two five-card suits, open the higher-ranking.

7] 16 points. (14 HCP plus 2 for singleton club.) Open 1 ♠. With three biddable four card suits, bid the suit below the singleton. In this case, spades is the suit below (around the corner from) clubs.

8] 16 points. (13 HCP plus 3 for void in spades). Open 1 ◇, bidding the longest suit first.

9]   15 points. (14 HCP plus 1 for doubleton diamond.) Open
1 ♣, your three-card minor. With no biddable four-card
suit, you have no other choice.

10]   21 points. (19 HCP plus 1 for each doubleton.) Bid 1 ♡.
This is maximum strength for an opening bid at the
one-level. With 1 more point, you would open at the
two-level. (To be explained in Lesson 9.)

Lesson 7: responding to the opening bid

Now, you are going to be the partner of the opening bidder – the *responder*. As opener's partner, responder should make some bid if he has 6 points or more. Except when raising partner's suit, these 6 points should be in high cards. If your response is a raise, you may count distributional points for shortness in order to avoid passing.

Why the 6-point minimum for a response?

— To raise partner's suit

There are two main reasons why responder should bid with as few as 6 points when opener bids one in a suit. First: Since opener may have as much as 20 points, if you hold 6 your side may have the total of 26 needed to bid game. Second: If responder's hand has no support for opener's suit, some other contract may be reached at which the combined hands may have greater trick-winning power. (Another reason – making it more difficult for the opponents to come into the bidding cheaply – will become apparent when we come to Lesson 10, "Competitive Bidding.") So you should try to make some "chance-giving bid". But if you hold only 6 to 8 points, and the intervening player takes some action, it is no longer necessary to bid in order to give partner a second chance. In this case you would be making what is called a *"free bid"* and your partner, the opener, will count on you for at least 9 or 10 points.

Responder's choice of actions.

The responder may give several types of answer to the opening bid, depending on his hand. These include:
- – Pass: 0 to 5 points;
- – Raise: 6 to 9–10 points;
- – Bid a suit of his own: 7 to 15 points;
- – Bid 1 notrump: 6 to 10 points.

We have already seen why responder should try not to pass.

Valuing responder's hand

High cards count as usual, A-4, K-3, Q-2, J-1, except that responder may add 1 point to a high card in opener's suit if he is not already counting 4 points in that suit. Thus an ace never counts more than 4, but a king counts 4; a queen counts 3; a jack counts 2, if it is not accompanied by a higher honor.

Distributional points count as usual except:
1. When holding four or more cards in opener's suit, responder:
   - – counts 3 points for a singleton (instead of 2)
   - – counts 5 points for a void (instead of 3)
2. Do not count distributional points for shortness in opener's suit.
3. Remember, short suits are not counted for notrump bids.
   Examples (opener bids 1 ♡):

a]	HCP	Dist.	b]	HCP	Dist.
♠ K 3 2	3	–	♠ K 3 2	3	–
♡ Q 8 6 5	3	–	♡ Q J 2	4	–
◇ 9 8	0	1	◇ 9 8 7 6	0	–
♣ 9 7 6 5	0	–	♣ 9 7 5	0	–
	6	1		7	0

		HCP	Dist.			HCP	Dist.
c]	♠ K 3 2	3	–	d]	♠ A J 5 4	5	–
	♡ K J 5 4	4	–		♡ 7 5	0	–
	◇ 9 8 7	0	–		◇ K 9 8 7	3	–
	♠ 8 7 2	0	–		♣ 8 7 2	0	–
		7	0			8	0

		HCP	Dist.
e]	♠ K Q 5 4	5	–
	♡ 7 5 3	0	–
	◇ K 9 8 7	3	–
	♣ 8 7	–	1
		8	1

a) shows the increased value of the ♡ Q, opener's suit. b) Also shows increased high card value, but only 1 point is added (to the higher honor). c) No addition for high card value, since responder is already counting 4. d) The doubleton has no distributional value because it is in partner's suit. e) The doubleton club is worth 1 point, even though you do not intend to support partner's suit.

Why a "fit" adds values.

The reason a *fit* increases the distributional value of a hand is that it indicates the presence of a playable trump suit. As a general rule, a trump suit of only seven cards in the combined hands of the partnership is not enough, because the opponents hold nearly as many trumps (six) as the declarer. With eight trumps, however, declarer usually can draw the opposing trumps in three rounds and still have trumps to deal with the enemy's high cards or long cards in his short suits. Or, if one partner has a singleton in a side suit and four trumps, his hand will be able to win additional tricks by ruffing at least one, probably two, and perhaps even three rounds of his short suit.

Similarly, an honor in partner's suit is likely to be more valuable because it is more certain to win a trick, or at least to prevent the opponents from winning tricks. The queen of a side suit may or may not win a trick. The queen of the trump suit – the suit in which partner is more likely to hold high cards – is more likely both to win a trick and to prevent the opponents from winning a trick which would have to be lost if that queen were missing.

For example, suppose opener bids 1 ♠ and responder holds:

> ♠ Q J 9 2
> ♡ 8
> ◇ J 10 4 3
> ♣ A 10 8 4

He can diagnose a fit at once, because opener must have at least four spades for his major suit opening. The singleton heart thus becomes worth 3 points instead of 2; and Q–J of spades are promoted 1 point to 4. But if the opening bid were 1 ♡, responder's hand would be worth four points fewer. The Q–J of spades would be worth only 3 HCP; the singleton heart would be valueless because shortness in partner's suit does not count.

Responder's choice of bids

With from 6 to 9 points; responder may:

1. Raise opener's suit from 1 to 2. (Occasionally, a single raise may include as many as 10 points.)

2. Bid 1 NT, lacking support for partner's suit.

3. Bid 1 in a new (higher-ranking) suit. If the suit is lower-ranking, responder should bid 1 NT.

With from 10 to 12 points, responder may:

Make a minimum response of 1 or, if necessary, 2 in a new suit.

a]	♠ A 10 7 4	b]	♠ 7 4	c]	♠ A Q 7 6 5
	♡ 9 8 6		♡ A 6 3		♡ A 6 3
	◇ A Q 2		◇ A Q 7 6 5		◇ 7 4
	♣ 7 5 2		♣ J 7 4		♣ J 7 4

a) Bid 1 ♠ over 1 ♡, 1 ◇, or 1 ♣.

b) Bid 2 ◇ over 1 ♡ or 1 ♠. Over 1 ♡, even though

responder has ♡ A 6 3, he should not bid 2 ♡, which would
show a maximum of 10 points. (But bid only 1 ◇ in response to
1 ♣.)

c) Bid 1 ♠, NOT 2 ♠, over any opening suit bid. 2 ♠ would
be a jump bid and would show at least 17 HCP.

With 13 points or more, responder may:

– Jump raise opener's suit (forcing to game), showing 13–15
points and four or more cards in partner's suit, preferably
headed by an honor if only four. For example, over 1 ♡,
responder bids 3 ♡ with:

> ♠ K 2
> ♡ Q 4 3 2
> ◇ J 9 6 2
> ♣ A Q J

– Jump in NT.
– Respond 2 NT (forcing, with 13, 14, 15)
– Respond 3 NT (not forcing, with 16, 17, 18)
– Bid a new suit, (forcing) with fewer than 19.

With 17 points or more, responder may:

– Jump in a new suit, skipping 1 level. e.g., over 1 ♡:

a]	b]
♠ K 8 3	♠ A K Q 10 9 5
♡ A Q 6 5	♡ 10 5
◇ A Q J 8 5	◇ A K 7
♣ 6	♣ K J

a) Bid 3 ◇. Responder has excellent support for opener's hearts
but is too strong to bid 3 ♡ (16 HCP plus 3 for singleton club.)

You have an excellent fit at hearts. If opener's hand fits well,
he may be able to make a slam (usually requiring 33 points or
more) even if he has only 14 to 15 points. For example, opener
may hold:

I.	II.
♠ A Q 2	♠ Q 10 2
♡ K J 10 8	♡ K J 9 7 4
◇ K 10 5	◇ K 10
♣ J 9 7	♣ A 9 5

Playing at 6 ♡, with hand I, opener will lose only one club
trick. With hand II, opener will lose only one spade trick. His

other losing spade can be discarded on responder's good diamonds, and the opponents cannot win a club trick because your hand will be able to trump the second round of clubs.

b) Bid 2 ♠. Although lacking heart support, responder has a self-sufficient spade suit and 20 HCP, plus 1 for the doubleton club.

Since skip bids (exactly one level higher than necessary in a new suit) are forcing to game, they may be used with hands of unlimited strength. Partner must keep on bidding until game, or a satisfactory penalty double of the opponents, has been reached. But beware of double jump bids. Such bids are not stronger than a single jump; in fact, they are weaker.

Jump to four of opener's major suit. With about 10 to 12 points, including points for distribution. Much of this strength will be in distributional points, i.e.:

a]		b]	
♠	A Q 10 8 3 2	♠	5 4
♡	5	♡	Q J 10 9 4 2
◇	Q 10 9 7	◇	A J 4
♣	3 2	♣	5 2

a) Respond 4 ♠ to 1 ♠. (8 HCP, 4 distributional points. Remember, singletons are worth 3 when supporting partner's suit.)

b) Respond 4 ♡ to 1 ♡. (9 HCP – remember, responder adds 1 point for Q–J in opener's suit – plus 1 for each of the two doubletons.)

Jumps to game are NOT strong bids. You hope to make game, but if you are set a trick or two, you may have prevented the opponents from bidding and making a game.

Responses in a new suit are forcing

All single-jump bids are forcing to game. It is easy to remember that these bids are forcing because they sound strong to the ear. There is one other forcing bid which may or may not be strong, and is not forcing to game. That is the bid of a new suit by responder.

If responder bids a new suit at the one-level, it may range from 6 to 16 points. If responder bids a new suit at the two-level, it may range from 10 to 16 points. These non-jump responses do not sound strong, but they are, nevertheless, forcing *for one round*. Whether they are based on strong hands or minimums will become clear at responder's next turn.

The only responses that are not forcing – that is, do not require opener to make another bid – are a single raise of opener's suit and a response of 1 NT. And, of course, a pass. Each of these responses limits the responder's hand; any rebid by the opener is entirely voluntary, and based on the knowledge that responder's strength is limited.

The chart that follows summarizes the weak (non-forcing) and strong (forcing) bids we have covered. The letter to the left of the various bids indicates the illustrative hand beneath the chart.

WEAK RESPONSES	Points
a) Pass	0–5
b) Single Raise	6–9
c) 1 NT	6–9

STRONG RESPONSES	Points
d) Jump Raise	13–15
e) Jump to 2 NT	13–15
f) Jump in new suit	17 plus
g) Jump to 3 NT	16–18

WIDE RANGE RESPONSES	Points
h) New suit at the 1-level	6–16
i) New suit at the 2-level	10–16

Assuming that opener bids 1 ♡, these are examples of the hands responder might have to make the response indicated by the corresponding letter in the table above.

a] ♠ J 8 7 5 ♡ 4 3 ◇ J 1 0 7 5 2 ♣ J 8
b] ♠ A J 5 ♡ 8 7 6 5 ◇ 1 0 9 ♣ Q 8 7 2
c] ♠ Q J 1 0 ♡ 6 ◇ Q J 6 4 2 ♣ J 1 0 8 7
d] ♠ A 6 ♡ K J 3 2 ◇ A 7 5 2 ♣ J 3 2
e] ♠ K J 1 0 ♡ J 9 ◇ A J 4 3 ♣ K J 8 6
f] ♠ A 3 ♡ K 7 ◇ K Q 1 0 9 8 2 ♣ A J 9
g] ♠ K 7 3 ♡ Q 5 3 ◇ A Q 1 0 ♣ K Q 9 8
h] 1. ♠ K J 9 6   2 ♠ A Q 9 6
       ♡ 4 3   ♡ Q 3
       ◇ K 7 6 2   ◇ A K 7 6
       ♣ 8 7 5   ♣ 6 5 4

With either hand, respond 1 ♠. Hand 2 is strong enough in
high cards to bid 2 ◇, but the guiding principle is that, with
more than one biddable four-card suit, bid the cheapest first. (It
is cheaper to bid 1 ♠ than 2 ◇. Besides, if you find a fit in
spades, you need to bid only 4 ♠ to score a game.)

i] 1. ♠ K 8   2. ♠ A 8
       ♡ 1 0 7   ♡ 8 7
       ◇ Q 1 0 9   ◇ A Q 1 0 9
       ♣ K Q 9 7 5 3   ♣ K J 7 5 4

1. **Bid 2 ♣**. You have just enough (10 points in high cards) to bid
a new suit at the two-level.
2. **Bid 2 ♣**. With more than one suit, bid the longer first.

You will notice that there is a considerable discrepancy in
strength between the two examples given for h) and i). That is
why it is always better for responder to select a bid that limits
his strength clearly whenever such a bid is available. But how
do you distinguish between the stronger and the weaker
responses when you make a wide-ranging bid? The answer will
appear when we discuss *rebids* in Lesson 8. Meanwhile, do not
worry about this.

All that it is necessary to remember is that both wide-range
responses and strong responses are forcing and the opener
must bid again.

Responder has two or more suits

Responder's choice of which of two or three suits to bid first is usually decided by the same rules that govern opener:

With suits of unequal length, bid the longer.

With suits of equal length, bid the higher ranking.

However, sometimes this choice is modified by the point count requirements shown in the foregoing chart. Sometimes responder cannot bid his longer suit first because he lacks sufficient points to bid it at the two-level. For example:

> ♠ A J 8 6
> ♡ 4 2
> ◊ Q J 9 7 6
> ♣ 4 2

If opener has bid 1 ♡, responder cannot show his longer suit first because his hand does not count the minimum of 10 points required for a bid of a new suit at the two-level. (Remember, he cannot count for shortage in opener's suit.) He therefore responds 1 ♠, just as he would do if he held one fewer diamond. However, if opener's bid were 1 ♣, responder would show the longer suit first, bidding 1 ◊.

Or suppose opener bids 1 ◊ and responder holds:

a]	b]	c]
♠ K J 6 2	♠ K Q 6 2	♠ A Q 10 5
♡ Q J 9 4	♡ Q J 9 2	♡ K Q 9 7
◊ –	◊ 5 2	◊ 5 2
♣ Q 9 8 4 2	♣ J 7 2	♣ K 7 6

With hands a) and b), responder must choose the cheapest suit, not the longest or the highest ranking. With c) he responds 1 ♠ and will later bid hearts.

The simplest way to decide when to depart from the general rule is to count points. If responder's hand does not count above 10 points, he makes the cheapest bid, expecting to bid only once unless partner makes a strong rebid. If responder has 11 or 12 points, he follows the general rule because he is strong enough to bid twice.

For example:

d] ♠ A Q J 2   e] ♠ A Q 4 3
    ♡ J 4   ♡ 5 4
    ◇ A 10 8 7 6   ◇ K 7 6 3 2
    ♣ 5 4   ♣ 5 4

Opener bids 1 ♡. With hand d) responder is strong enough to make two bids (12 points) so he bids 2 ◇; then if opportunity offers, he will bid spades later. With e), however, he has only 10 points and should respond 1 ♠.

Remember, responder still needs at least 6 points to make any response. He must pass opener's 1 ♡ opening with:

f] ♠ J 8 6 5 2
    ♡ 5 4
    ◇ Q 9 7 6 4
    ♣ 5

Responding to notrump openings

Since an opening bid of 1 NT shows 16 to 18 HCP in a balanced hand, responder needs 8 to 10 points to bring the partnership's total to the 26 usually needed for game.

Distributional points count when responder has a long suit. He can usually expect from opener support for his suit and the high cards needed to prevent the opponents from quickly winning enough tricks to defeat a game contract. Here, in brief, is a summary of requirements for the responses to notrump openings.

Responses to 1 NT

7 points or fewer. Pass with a balanced hand but bid two of a long suit with a holding that will not play well at notrump. For example:

a] ♠ 6
    ♡ 9 4
    ◇ Q 8 7 6 5 4
    ♣ Q 10 5 2

b] ♠ J 10 9 7 6
    ♡ 2
    ◇ Q 4 3
    ♣ Q 9 5 2

With a), respond 2 ◇. With b), respond 2 ♠.

Responder is not trying to get to game; he is merely showing a hand that is likely to play one trick better, at least, if played in his long suit. Opener should recognize that a minimum suit takeout of his 1 NT opening is NOT an encouraging bid.

8 or 9 HCP (balanced hand). Bid two notrump. If opener has 16, he will pass; if he has a maximum, he will carry on to game. Responder should never bid only two of a suit with this much strength. He should either bid 2 NT, or, with an unbalanced hand (singleton or void) he may skip the bid to 3 of his suit.

10 to 14 points: Respond 3 NT with a balanced hand; three of a long suit, forcing, with an unbalanced hand.

15 or 16 points: Respond 4 NT with a balanced hand; three of a long suit with an unbalanced hand. If opener has better than a minimum the combined hands contain 33 points and justify bidding a small slam.

17 points: Jump to 6 NT, or skip to 3 of a long suit. You will insist on a slam because the combined hands must total at least 33 points.

With a seven-card or longer major: Skip to game in the major, even if responder has no more than 5 points. This is NOT a strong bid.

Quiz No. 7

1] Opener bids 1 ♠. Count the points in this responding hand:
    ♠ 9 8 7 6
    ♡ K 3
    ◇ Q 6 5 4
    ♣ Q J 8

2]   Opener bids 1 ♠. Responder holds:

    ♠ A J
    ♡ 9 8 7 6 4
    ◇ K 7 6 5
    ♣ 9 8

What should he respond?   *1 NT*

need 10 pts to go to 3 level.

3]   Opener bids 1 ♣. What should responder bid, holding:

    ♠ K J 7 6 5
    ♡ Q 2
    ◇ A Q 7 5 3
    ♣ 7

12 pts   *1 ♠*

4]   Opener bids 1 ◇. What is the response with:

    ♠ K Q 9 5
    ♡ K Q J 6
    ◇ Q 7
    ♣ 5 4 3

13 pts   *1 ♠*

5]   Opener bids 1 ♠. What should responder bid with:

    ♠ K 10 8 7
    ♡ 6 4 3
    ◇ Q J 9 8 7
    ♣ 3

10 pts   *2 ♠* *– extra pt for K ♠*

singleton – 3 pts

6]   Opener bids 1 ♣. What should responder bid with:

    ♠ A Q
    ♡ Q J 10
    ◇ K J 6 5
    ♣ Q 10 8 2

15 pts   *2 NT*

7]   Which is the stronger response to a 1 ♡ opening: 3 ♡ or
    4 ♡?   *3 ♡ – shows 13-15 pts*

8]   In responding to 1 NT, is two of a suit forcing?

9]   Opener bids 1 NT. What should responder bid, holding:

11 pts   ♠ K J 10 9 7 5   *K extra pts ; 6 cards extra* *1 ♠*
singleton – 3   ♡ 8
    ◇ Q J 10
    ♣ 10 9 8 2

10]   Opener bids 1 NT. What should responder bid, holding:

    ♠ J 2
    ♡ Q 8   *2 ◇*
    ◇ J 9 8 7 6
    ♣ 10 9 8 2

4 HCP

Answers to Quiz No. 7

1] **9 points**; 8 HCP + 1 point for the doubleton heart. There is a guaranteed fit in spades. (The best response is 2 ♠.)

2] 1 NT. Responder's hand lacks the 10 points needed to bid a new suit at the two-level, or enough spades to raise.

3] 1 ♠. With two five-card suits, start with the higher ranking.

4] 1 ♠. When responding with two (or more) four-card suits, start with the higher ranking if you hold 11 HCP or more.

5] 2 ♠. Your hand is worth 10 points in support of spades; 7 HCP (you upgrade the spade King) plus 3 for the singleton club.

6] **2 NT**. With 15 points (all HCP) your alternative would be to jump to 3 ♣, but that should promise five-card support. Besides, game in notrump (nine tricks) is easier than game in clubs (eleven tricks).

7] 3 ♡ – a forcing bid showing excellent support and 13–15 HCP. 4 ♡ is a shutout bid, based largely on distributional values with fewer HCP.

8] **No**. A bid of 2 in a suit is weak. It simply says that the responder expects his hand to be of greater value if played in his long suit.

9] 4 ♠. Responder's hand is worth 11 points – 8 HCP plus 3 for the singleton heart. For suit bids facing a 1 NT opening, distributional points are counted the same as for a raise of opener's suit. Opener's 1 NT guarantees at least two cards in every suit. There are more than 26 points in the combined hands.

10] **Bid 2 ◇**. Although your hand is worth only 4 HCP, it should be able to make at least one more trick in diamonds than at a notrump contract.

Lesson 8: The bidding continues: rebids by opener and responder

Until now, you have been playing a sort of solitaire bridge, in which you have considered only the bidding of a single player – either the opener or responder. We are ready now to consider the further progress of the auction for the right to name the final contract, with the object of reaching game or slam or of stopping at a safe level, before your side runs the risk of incurring a heavy penalty. You are going to bid as a member of a partnership, exchanging additional information to determine two important questions:

1. What is the best declaration (suit or notrump) for the combined hands?

2. How high you should go: part score, game or slam?

The first question is often answered by opener's bid and his partner's first response. When a fit is revealed by responder's raise, or by his bid of a suit for which opener has excellent support, you have found the probable place at which the hand should be played.

The second question requires the answer to the first, plus a gauge of the trick-taking value of the combined hands. The guide is:

With fewer than 26 points combined, *play below game.*

With at least 26 points combined, *play in game.*

With at least 33 points combined, *consider a small slam.*

With at least 37 points combined, *aim toward a grand slam.*

Bear in mind, however, that the key figures 26, 33 and 37 are a guide, not a law. Game will sometimes be made on 22 points and may be set though the combined hands count 28. *Controls:* the ability to win the first or second trick in a suit, are the deciding factor.

The more unbalanced the hands, the more frequent will be the exceptions to these guides. When freak hands are held, it is important to remember the earlier lessons in how tricks are won.

Limit bids: Hands that define strength at once.

Notrump opening bids are the easiest on which the partnership can answer both questions: Where? How high?

When the opening bid is 1 NT (16 to 18 HCP, balanced hand), responder knows that unless he holds *at least* 8 points, game is probably out of reach. He can pass, or, if his hand is weak but includes a long suit, he can make a minimum suit takeout which *opener is expected to pass.* With 8 or 9 points, responder bids 2 NT and opener passes unless he has better than the minimum 16. With 10-plus points, responder bids 3 NT, or forces by jumping to three of a long suit. With 15 or 16 points, responder bids 4 NT. With a total that will surely put the combined hands at least at or above the 33 mark, responder bids 6 NT; rarely, with 21 or more points, responder may jump directly to 7 NT. But with only 21, responder should have good intermediate cards that will bolster the trick-taking power of several suits: tens and nines under higher honors.

Limit raises by opener or responder: Responder's single raise or bid of 1 NT shows 7 to 10 points. Opener's rebid of 1 NT: 13 to 15 points. Opener's minimum rebid of his own suit: 13 to 15.

Combining these maximums, it is clear that the partnership cannot hold 26 points. For example:

a) OPENER	RESPONDER
♠ Q J 9 4 2	♠ K 10 8 7
♡ A 2	♡ 7 6
◇ K 4 3	◇ J 10 7
♣ A 6 5	♣ K 8 7 3

OPENER	OPP.	RESPONDER	OPP.
1 ♠	(Pass)	2 ♠	(Pass)
Pass			

Opener counts a maximum of 24 points. He will surely lose at least one trick in every suit. There is no advantage to bidding 3 ♠ even if it can be made. He will score the same 90 points, 60 below the line and 30 above. But if he is set, he will lose not only the 60 points below the line, plus the penalty of 50 or 100 above, but also the advantage of having a part score to help toward scoring game on a subsequent hand.

b) OPENER
   ♠ Q J 9 4
   ♡ K 10 8 3
   ◇ K 4
   ♣ A 6 5

OPENER	OPP.
1 ♠	(Pass)
	(Pass)

RESPONDER
   ♠ 10 6
   ♡ Q 9 7
   ◇ Q 9 8 3
   ♣ K 9 7 3

RESPONDER	OPP.
1 NT	(Pass)

Declarer must surely lose two spades, one heart and one diamond in top cards alone. A 2 ♡ rebid by opener is unwarranted. Opener's hand is suited to NT play and he knows that his side cannot have more than 22 – 23 points in high cards, and possibly might have only 19.

c) OPENER
   ♠ J 6
   ♡ A k J 5 4 2
   ◇ A 5
   ♣ 7 5 3

OPENER	OPP.
1 ♡	(Pass)
2 ♡	(Pass)

	RESPONDER	RESPONDER	OPP.
	♠ Q 10 4	1 NT	(Pass)
	♡ 8 3	Pass	(Pass)
	◇ Q 9 8 4		
	♣ K Q 6 4		

Opener bids 2 ♡ in preference to playing at 1 NT, although he knows that his side's total points cannot exceed 23 in high cards and may be less. Depending on the location of the opponent's cards, he might even be set at 2 ♡, but the suit contract is probably safer. Responder knows that if opener had a stronger hand he would have made a stronger rebid, so he passes.

When opener *has* a stronger hand, he may not immediately know how high his side can bid. For example:

d)	OPENER	OPENER	(Opp.)
	♠ K 6	1 ♡	(Pass)
16 pts.	♡ A K Q 9 4 2	3 ♡	(Pass)
	◇ 10 5		
	♣ A 5 2		

	RESPONDER	RESPONDER	(Opp.)
	♠ Q 10 4	1 NT	(Pass)
	♡ 8 3	3 NT	
	◇ Q 9 8 4		
	♣ K Q 6 4		

With better than a minimum (9 points instead of only 6) after opener has shown the strength of his hand by jump rebidding his suit (not forcing but strongly encouraging) responder rebids 3 NT, having the other three suits reasonably well guarded. If opener held a singleton spade, he might return to 4 ♡. As it is, he is content to play 3 NT, which should be safe even if hearts break badly – 4-1).

e) OPENER	e 1] RESPONDER	e 2] RESPONDER
♠ K 6 2	♠ Q 10 9	♠ Q 9 2
♡ A K 7 5 4	♡ 8 2	♡ 8 2
◇ A 10	◇ Q 9 8 4	◇ Q 9 8 4
♣ A 5 2	♣ K Q 6 4	♣ Q 7 6 4

1 ♡	(Pass)	1 NT	or	1 NT	(Pass)
2 NT	(Pass)	3 NT		Pass	

Opener's raise to 2 NT shows a balanced hand with 17 to 19 points. If responder has better than the minimum 6, he bids 3 NT. With e2) however, he should pass 2 NT.

Strengthen opener's hand above by 2 HCP, adding either the ♡ Q or the ◇ J and ♠ J for example, and opener should jump to 3 NT. He counts on responder to produce a minimum of 6 HCP and thus the partnership total is at least 26, but is surely not more than 30.

Using the key numbers 26, 33 and 37, whenever a playable contract has been found, the partner who possesses this information acts to reach the game or slam suggested by the combined total.

Forcing responses

Forcing responses fall into two categories:

1. Responder's bid of a new suit, forcing for one round. (For example: 1 ♡-1 ♠; 1 ♣ - 1 of any suit; 1 ♡-2 ♣ or 2 ◇; 1 ♠ - 2 of any suit.)

2. Jumps to 2 NT; single jump raises (1 ◇ - 3 ◇; 1 ♠-3 ♠); and jump responses in new suits (1 ♡ - 2 ♠, or 3 ♣ or 3 ◇); 1 ♠ - 3 of any suit), are forcing to game. The jump to 2 NT and the single jump raise are limited (13 to 15 points). The jump in a new suit is unlimited as to the top range and is usually made with a possible slam in mind if opener has better than a minimum. This is because any new suit response would be forcing and responder can show his full strength with his next bid.

The jump to 3 NT is not forcing. It shows a balanced hand of

16, 17 or 18 points, on a hand that contains no singleton *or* doubleton. Opener may rebid if his total indicates the probable possession of a combined 33 points and therefore a possible slam.

Finding a fit

When responder has made a one-round forcing bid by showing a new suit, he may or may not be expecting to raise /opener's suit later. Opener should:
1. Announce a fit in responder's suit, either by a single or a jump raise.
2. Rebid a six-card suit or a strong five-card suit.
3. Bid a new suit.
4. Jump in a new suit (forcing).
5. Bid the minimum number of notrump necessary to answer responder's force.
6. Jump rebid in notrump.

Responder's rebid

If opener's rebid has shown a minimum hand, responder should bid again only if he has additional values, or if he is still seeking to find a possible fit.

OPENER	RESPONDER
♠ 5	♠ K J 10 4 2
♡ A K 7 6 4	♡ J 2
◇ K J 5	◇ A Q 9 4 2
♣ A Q 6 2	♣ 3

OPENER	RESPONDER
1 ♡	1 ♠
2 ♣	2 ◇

Responder has no fit with either of partner's suits and shows better than minimum values by bidding 2 ◇. He hopes that opener can raise diamonds, show some slight support for spades, or bid notrump. With the example hands, opener raises to 3 ◇ and 5 ◇ is reached.

If opener held:

— ♠ A 3 or ♠ Q 3, or three low spades, he would jump in partner's first suit, bidding 3 ♠.

— if, in addition to these spade holdings, opener held a supporting honor in diamonds, he would jump to 4 ♠.

With no support for either of responder's suits, opener should rebid 2 ♡, and responder should pass.

Similarly, if responder held a weaker hand with equal or better hearts than clubs, he would not show diamonds but would simply return to opener's first bid suit by bidding 2 ♡.

WARNING: When it is apparent that no fit exists, *sign off* at the cheapest level in whichever suit offers the best fit. Do not flee to notrump with ill-fitting weak hands. Notrump contracts depend upon:

1. Stoppers in all suits, and, if game is to be made:

2. The essential minimum number of high card points – 26; or

3. A ready source of tricks, such as a solid suit, or cards in partner's long suit which suggest that his suit will produce the necessary tricks.

Whenever you are considering a notrump declaration on a misfit hand, ask yourself where the tricks are coming from.

Revaluation

The alert student will have observed that there is a constant revaluation taking place with each new bid. When a fit is found by responder's bid of a new suit, opener is able to revalue singletons and voids as if he were the responding hand. The same process takes place for responder if opener's second bid reveals a newly found fit. For example:

RESPONDER
♠ 8
♡ Q J 9 7 2
◇ Q 10 9 4
♣ A 10 8

If opener's bid was 1 ♠, responder's hand is worth only his 9 HCP and, since he is not strong enough to respond at the two-level, which requires a minimum of 10 points, he responds 1 NT. But if opener next bids 2 ♡, responder's hand adds 3 for his singleton spade and his ♡ Q-J become worth 4 points instead of 3. Responder's hand is now worth 13 points and he should jump to 4 ♡ (13 plus 13 equals 26 – the magic number).

The same is true of opener's hand. Suppose he opens 1 ♣ with:

♠ 8 2
♡ K 10 8 3
◇ A 9
♣ A K 6 5 4

If responder bids 1 ♠, opener must rebid 1 NT. But if responder's bid was 1 ♡, opener's hand becomes worth 3 extra points: 1 more for each doubleton (which could not be counted for a NT bid) and 1 more for the promotion of the ♡ K (partner's suit) from 3 to 4. His total if hearts becomes the final declaration is now 17 points and he can afford to raise to 3 ♡ – not forcing but strongly encouraging.

After a raise: When responder's first bid is a raise, opener's *long suit* takes on immediate added values:
– Opener adds 1 point for a fifth trump.
– Opener adds 2 points for a sixth and each additional trump.

Responder adds points in the same way when opener's first rebid is a raise of responder's five-card or longer suit.

If these added points bring the known *minimum* total to 23 to 25 points, the player who has first bid the suit rebids to the three-level, so that if partner has added values he will be encouraged to bid for game.

If these added points bring the known *minimum* total to 26 points, the player who can count the combined values to this total goes at once to game.

Reverse Bids

With the foregoing hand, why did not opener rebid 2 ♡ instead of 1 NT over 1 ♠? The answer is that this would be a *reverse* – a strong hand because, if partner prefers opener's first suit, he may have to bid clubs at the three-level.

A reverse – that is bidding a higher ranking suit after a lower-ranking one – unless it can only be done at the one-level shows a very good hand, approximately 18-19 points. Although this is not an inviolable force, when you reverse you are expecting partner to bid again and he should pass only if he has shaded his initial response because he did not like your first suit.

Examples: Opener bids 1 ♣ and responder bids 1 ♠ or 1 NT:

	a]		b]	
	♠ 4 3		♠ 4 3	
	♡ A Q J 4		♡ K J 9 7	
	◊ K 2		◊ K 2	
	♣ A K J 8 7		♣ A Q J 8 7	

With a), rebid 2 ♡; you are strong enough for a reverse.

With b), rebid 2 ♣. Your hand is not strong enough for a reverse.

However, if responder's bid was 1 ◊, you may bid 1 ♡ with either a) or b). A bid of a higher ranking suit *at the one-level* is not considered a reverse. Indeed, it may not mean that you have more clubs than hearts. For example:

♠ Q 10 2
♡ K J 9 7
◊ 6 5
♣ A K Q 8

This hand is a correct opening bid of 1 ♣ (the suit below your shortest suit) and a rebid of 1 ♡ over 1 ◇. If partner bids 1 ♠, you will raise to 2 ♠. If partner bids 1 NT you will pass.

Free bids and rebids

When an opponent bids or doubles opener's bid, responder is freed from the obligation to keep the bidding open with as few as 6 points. Opener will have a chance to bid again if responder passes.

The same is true when opener's right hand opponent comes into the bidding after responder's forcing response. Opener is no longer required to keep the bidding open because responder will have another opportunity to bid if he wishes to. For example:

OPENER	OPP.	RESPONDER	OPP.
1 ◇	Pass	1 ♡	1 ♠
?			

Without the 1 ♠ overcall, opener is forced to bid again. Given the overcall, however, if opener makes any free rebid he is showing additional values. These may be in high cards or in distribution:

a] ♠ A 4 2   b] ♠ K 4   c] ♠ 7
    ♡ Q 2   ♡ K 7 6 3   ♡ Q 2
    ◇ A K 7 6 5   ◇ A K 7 6 5   ◇ A K 7 6 5
    ♣ Q 8 3   ♣ 8 7   ♣ A J 10 8 7

With a), opener passes the 1 ♠ bid, indicating a minimum opening and no great support for partner.

With b) opener raises freely. Although his hand is still a minimum in high cards, with b) the value of the ♡K (his partner's suit) is now 4 points, and the ♠ K is promoted in value since it is behind the spade bidder, who very probably holds the ♠ A, making it much more likely that the ♠ K will win a trick. Opener rebids 2 ♡.

With c) opener rebids 2 ♣ because he is hoping to find a fit in his second suit. He is also able to add a point to the value of his ♡ Q, even though he is not planning to play in hearts.

In this situation, remember that although responder's heart bid was forcing it should not be treated as more than a 6-point minimum until responder's next action indicates otherwise.

Suppose, however, that the bidding had been:

OPENER	OPP.	RESPONDER	OPP.
1 ◇	1 ♡	1 ♠	Pass

Responder's 1 ♠ bid is forcing for one round, and opener must bid again. Returning to the example hands previously shown:

With a) his choice would be 2 ♠. Responder's hand is better than a minimum and presumably, for his free bid, he has a five-card suit.

With b), opener, being forced to bid again, should rebid 1 NT to indicate his heart stopper and caution responder against expecting spade support.

With c), opener rebids 2 ♣, showing his distribution and warning that he does not have spade support or a heart stopper; i.e., that the hands may be a misfit unless responder can support one of opener's suits.

In a student's text, it is not desirable to cover all the possible situations, but the following quiz will be additionally informative and at the same time test your understanding of this lesson.

Quiz No. 8

1] You open 1 ♡ and partner responds 2 ♡.

♠ K 7
♡ K J 7 6 4
◇ A J 7 6 4
♣ 3

What is your hand worth at this point?

2] You open 1 ♣ and partner responds 1 ♡. You hold:

♠ A Q 4
♡ K 9 8 7
◇ 10
♣ A J 8 7 5

Re-evaluate your hand.

3] You open 1 ♡ and partner raises to 2 ♡. You hold:

♠ K Q 7
♡ A J 9 8 6 2
◇ A Q 7 4
♣ —

What do you bid now?

4] This question, and those that follow are based upon your understanding of the following bidding:

YOU	OPPONENT	RESPONDER	OPPONENT
1 ♠	2 ♣	3 ◇	Pass
3 ♡	Pass	3 ♠	Pass
4 ♠	Pass	Pass	Pass

♠ A Q 9 8
♡ K Q J 6
◇ 7 2
♣ J 8 6

Your left hand opponent's overcall of 2 ♣ indicates a good club suit and from 10 to 12 points.

a) What is the significance of responder's bid of 3 ◇?

b) Why did you bid 3 ♡?

c) Explain partner's bid of 3 ♠.

d) Why did you bid 4 ♠ with only a four-card suit?

5] You hold:

♠ K J 5 4 2
♡ A Q 6 5 4
◇ K 3
♣ 2

The bidding has gone:

YOU	OPPONENT	PARTNER	OPPONENT
1 ♠	Pass	1 NT	Pass
2 ♡	Pass	4 ♡	Pass
?			

a) What is the significance of your **2** ♡ rebid?
b) What is the meaning of partner's jump to **4** ♡?
c) What do you bid now?

Answers to Quiz No. 8

1]   16 points – you add 1 point for the fifth heart. Partner's raise is limited to 9 (rarely 10 points). However, if he holds the necessary fillers for diamonds, there is still hope of game (let us say ♡ **Q** and ◇ **K 2**). You should express interest in going on by bidding **3** ◇, asking partner whether he has the "right" cards to be worth a game bid.

2] Your hand was worth 16 points when you opened with **1♣**; 14 in high cards and 2 for the singleton diamond. However, it is **now worth 18 points**: one additional point for your ♡ **K** because it is partner's suit; one additional point for the singleton because you are now raising partner's bid. You may bid **3** ♡, urging but not forcing. If partner has better than a minimum, he should go to game (**4** ♡).

3]   You are entitled to increase the estimated value of your trump holding by 1 point for the fifth and 2 for the sixth heart, once partner raises the suit. You also count 3 for the club void, so your hand is now worth about 22 points. Since partner's raise shows a minimum of 6 points, you jump to game (**4** ♡).

4] a) **Notice that this was a skip bid** of one more than necessary in a new suit. It is therefore very strong and forcing to game.

b) Because that is your natural rebid. You cannot rebid your four-card spade suit, nor can you bid notrump without a stopper in the club suit bid by the opponents.

c) Partner's bid of **3 ♠** shows delayed support. He probably has three or four spades headed by an honor. He must have excellent support and no club stopper or he would have rebid **4** ◇ or **3** NT.

d) Because you have no other bid available and you must keep bidding until game has been reached. You cannot raise partner's diamonds, nor can you bid NT without a club stopper.

5] a) **You are showing your second suit.** Your hand is not suitable to NT play and will be much more valuable if partner can support either of your suits. Your singleton and doubleton distributional points do not count at NT.

b) He has a hand that is short in spades but has good heart support, even if you have bid a four-card heart suit. He also has better than the minimum 6 points, especially in support of hearts.

c) Pass. The original notrump response limited your partner's values and there is no real hope that you will be able to make a slam.

Lesson **9**: **powerhouse hands and preemptive bids**

What does opener do when he has so strong a hand that he wants responder to bid even though he has fewer than 6 points? Here we come to an apparent contradiction, but a logical one.

It is not true that the more you have the higher your opening bid should be. In fact, there are two kinds of openings above the one-level, and the higher bid shows a weaker hand. Consider these examples:

a) ♠ –
   ♡ A K Q 8 4
   ◇ A K J 10 8
   ♣ K J 5

b) ♠ A K J 10 9 8 6 5
   ♡ –
   ◇ 9 2
   ♣ 10 9 3

With hand a), opener does not need to find 6 points in the responder's hand. Just the ♣ Q is enough to insure a game in whichever red suit responder can best support. The ◇ Q and the ♣ Q will probably produce a small slam. The ♣ A and five low cards in either hearts or diamonds will probably produce a grand slam.

If there were no bid that would guarantee a response from partner, opener would have to guess and hope. He might bid 4 ♡, 5 ◇, or even 6 ♡ or 6 ◇. But suppose he chooses the wrong suit for trumps, runs into a bad break and is set when the game or perhaps a slam could have been made at the other suit?

With hand b), however, opener knows he wants to play at

spades and he can afford to bid 4 ♠. If partner has the right cards, he will make it – perhaps more; the worst that can happen is that he will be set two tricks and the penalty will be lightened by his 100 honors. But see what happens if the holder of hand b) opens with 4 ♠ and an opponent holds hand a). The high opening bid has made life very difficult for the opponents. It is therefore called a *pre-emptive* bid – which we'll discuss further later in this lesson.

In order to show a really powerful hand like hand a) – too strong for an opening bid at the one-level – we open at the two-level. This two-bid begins where the one bids end; the minimum is 22 points. There is no maximum, so opening two-bids in a suit are *unlimited*. Of course, they are forcing. In fact, unless the two-bidder makes a minimum rebid of his suit on the next round, the two-bid is forcing to game. With a powerhouse hand, when deciding which suit to bid first, follow the rules for a one-bid; first bid the longer suit, or the higher ranking of two suits of equal length. Some illustrations of two-bids follow:

a) ♠ K Q J 6 5 3	b) ♠ –	c) ♠ A K Q
♡ A K 7	♡ A K Q 8 4	♡ A
◇ 9	◇ A K J 10 8	◇ A Q
♣ A K 9	♣ K J 5	♣ K Q 9 7 5 3 2
Open 2 ♠; a minimum	Open 2 ♡	Open 2 ♣ (unlimited)

EXCEPTION: An opening bid of 2 NT is a specialized two-bid showing a balanced hand and 22-24 points. Since this is the only two-bid with an upper limit, it is the only two-bid which is not forcing. Of course it is highly encouraging, but if responder knows that the partnership cannot have 26 points combined, he can and should pass.

An opening bid of 3 NT also shows a balanced hand, with a range of 25-27 points.

The negative response: 2 NT

Responder is forced to keep the bidding open opposite a suit two-bid, no matter what he holds. With 0-5 points responder bids 2 NT, *negative*. This bid does not promise balanced distribution as most notrump bids do; it is simply a warning that responder is very weak. Therefore, if opener is unwilling to play below game, he must either jump on his rebid or name a new suit, which continues to be forcing. Using our three sample two bids, let's see how opener would continue, assuming he received a negative 2 NT response.

a) ♠ K Q J 6 5 3   b) ♠ –   c) ♠ A K Q
   ♡ A K 7   ♡ A K Q 8 4   ♡ A
   ◇ 9   ◇ A K J 10 8   ◇ A Q
   ♣ A K 9   ♣ K J 5   ♣ K Q 9 7 5 3 2

With a), opener rebids 3 ♠; he has a minimum. If responder passes there is little fear of missing a game, since he has one loser in each suit. In terms of tricks, a two-bid usually contains at least nine winners, which means that responder will usually push to game if he thinks his hand is worth one trick.

With b), opener should rebid 3 ◇, descriptive and forcing. Game, even slam, is still possible, so the search for a fit continues.

With c), opener's best choice is to jump to 4 ♣. Remember, a simple rebid of 3 ♣ may be passed. Holding an almost certain game in his own hand opener must make a forcing bid.

Positive responses

Suppose now that responder has a useful hand, 6 points or more. He makes his natural response. If he has a biddable suit he names it; if he has support (three cards) for opener's suit, he raises. If he has a notrump type of hand, he must jump to 3 NT to show it since 2 NT means the negative. Note that after any of these natural *positive* responses, the partnership is committed to at least game; this is safe because there are 28 points minimum in the combined hands. Some typical positive responses follow: (assume opener bid 2 ♡)

d) ♠ 10 9	e) ♠ Q 10 8 6 2	f) ♠ A Q 6
♡ J 7 6	♡ 7	♡ –
◇ K Q 5 3	◇ Q J 6	◇ K J 7 6 4 3
♣ J 9 7 6	♣ Q J 5 2	♣ K 7 4 2
Respond 3 ♡	Respond 2 ♠	Respond 3 ◇
		(positives are unlimited)

Responses to 2 NT opening

Responding to a 2 NT opening presents one basic difference. Since 2 NT is limited and non-forcing, the most negative response is to pass (0-3 points). With 4 points or more, responder knows the partnership owns a minimum of 26, so he makes his natural bid which is forcing to game. Holding a balanced hand he raises notrump, holding a five-card or longer suit he names it. One important exception is this kind of hand:

> ♠ 8 7 6
> ♡ Q 3
> ◇ K J 10 6 4
> ♣ 10 9 2

Opposite a 2 NT opening the best response is 3 NT, not 3 ◇. 3 NT will be easier to make than 5 ◇; the long diamonds will produce tricks in both contracts, and in notrump declarer can afford two additional losers. The danger of responding 3 ◇ is that opener may raise to 4 ◇, blocking the partnership out of 3 NT.

With 3 points or fewer: Pass. Responder should not show a long suit unless prepared to bid for game.
With 4 to 7 points balanced: Bid 3 NT.
With 11 or 12 points: Jump to 6 NT

Responses to 3 NT opening

With fewer than 6 points: Pass. Any bid in response to 3 NT is a slam try.

(A method of finding a fit in a four-card major (a Stayman 2 ♣ bid in response to partner's 1 NT) will be discussed in Lesson 12.)

Pre-emptive bids

A pre-empt is a bid that skips several levels of the auction. It shows a long, strong suit in an otherwise weak hand. An opening pre-empt is made at the three-level or higher; it should contain a sizable number of tricks because it precludes any low-level contract. Unlike the two bid, where the tricks come from a great number of honor cards, the pre-emptor's tricks come almost exclusively from his trump suit.

The requirements for an opening pre-emptive bid at the three level are: 1) A very strong seven-card suit, 2) a hand worth six tricks if not vulnerable, seven tricks if vulnerable. The overall strength of the hand should not exceed 10 HCP, with the majority of the points concentrated in the long suit. Basically, a pre-empt is not based on point count but on trick-taking ability. (Remember the limitations of the point count tables on distributionally unbalanced hands.) A pre-empt is also a defensively oriented bid, in that one of its chief aims is to obstruct the opponents. Let's briefly examine the theory behind pre-empts, especially since it goes hand in hand with our method of learning bridge – the way tricks are won.

An ideal 3 ♠ opening, not vulnerable, is

♠ K Q J 9 8 5 2
♡ 6
♢ J 10 9
♣ 8 4

This hand is worth a likely six tricks in spades; if you are left to play 3 ♠ and partner contributes nothing you will be set three tricks. Though it may not appear so, this is a very worthwhile risk. In fact, if you aren't doubled by the opponents you stand to gain points! This paradox of gaining by losing can be explained by considering the defensive potential of the partnership hands.

A good pre-empt such as this one is worth next to nothing on defense. The only high-card strength carries little weight defensively because it is located in a long suit; at least one opponent is short in spades, ready to trump an early round. Outside of spades, if neither you nor your partner can contribute any tricks (which is how 3 ♠ may be set three), the opponents will be able to make virtually anything they bid – a game or even a slam. Thus, the pre-empt is a sound tactic, because it robs the enemy of several levels of bidding where they would be able to investigate their prospects. Instead of a nice leisurely auction, they must stab at a contract. They may undervalue their hands, missing a game or slam and saving you points. Or they may be goaded into overbidding and taking a set, converting a sure loss for your side into a small gain. Also, once in a while your partner will be in a position to double their blind stab (even though he is warned you will contribute little to the defense), scoring a huge gain.

Of course, the opponents won't always arrive at the wrong contract. But when they guess correctly, they simply get to the "normal" contract, the one they would have reached without the pre-empt, so nothing has been lost. Properly used, pre-empts will be a most potent weapon.

We have visualized how they make life difficult for the enemy; now let's see how they make life easy for partner.

Responding to pre-empts

Responding to pre-empts is based on evaluating top card winners – Aces and Kings, not points. Suppose partner opens 3 ♠ not vulnerable and you hold:

♠ A 4 3
♡ A 9 8 7 2
◇ 5
♣ A 9 7 6

You expect partner to provide six tricks and your hand is worth
four – the three Aces plus the trick partner will score by
trumping one of his low diamonds with one of your spades.
Playing the hand in your mind's eye you visualize that partner
will make all seven of his spades (your ace should solidify his
suit), your two aces, and one diamond ruffing trick. Therefore,
the proper response is 4 ♠. Counting tricks gives you the
answer, while counting points would dictate a pass since the
combined total is short of 26.

Suppose that partner opens 3 ♣ vulnerable. Because penalties are more severe when vulnerable, this pre-empt shows a
seven-winner hand, not six. You hold:

♠ K Q 2
♡ A 8 6 3 2
◇ A 9 7
♣ K 8

Your bid? Visualizing tricks, we place partner with the remaining high clubs, yielding seven winners in that suit plus the two
red Aces, or a minimum of nine winners in notrump. In a club
contract we predict ten winners (the same nine + one spade).
The correct bid, 3 NT, stands out.

Not vulnerable against vulnerable opponents, partner opens
the bidding with 3 ◇ and your right hand opponent passes. You
hold:

♠ 9 8 5 2
♡ 10
◇ K 9 6 5
♣ Q J 10 8

Calculating offensive tricks, we expect seven diamond winners
from partner plus one or two heart ruffing tricks in our hand.

Thus, if partner owns three hearts we will probably make 3 ◊ (one heart and only three black-suit losers); if partner has a doubleton heart, 3 ◊ should be set one trick (one heart and four black-suit losers). Calculating defensive tricks, our hand may produce one club trick, partner may score his presumed diamond Ace (although one opponent could easily be void), and partner may have a trick somewhere else. That's a total of three possible defensive tricks, all of them uncertain. The opponents surely have a fit in hearts. What do these calculations suggest? That the vulnerable opponents can score a game (at least) in hearts, winning the rubber. On the scoresheet that will amount to at least 820 points.

As responder you should leap to 5 ◊ immediately, exerting maximum pressure on the enemy. What can happen?

1) Your left-hand opponent may be deluded into thinking you have a strong hand and pass. Your side will pay a 100 or 150 point penalty for being set two or three tricks. Even if you are doubled you lose at most 500, still a substantial saving over the 820 you would pay if opponents make 4 ♡.

2) Deprived of bidding room to investigate, the opponents may arrive at the wrong suit or the wrong level and be set. Now your bold 5 ◊ bid has turned a large loss into a profit.

This is but one example of the imaginative ways that pre-empts can be exploited. As long as the opening three-bidder sticks to the basic requirements – a solid or nearly solid seven-card suit with little or no defensive prospects – responder can make deadly accurate assessments of the tricks either side will win. Properly exploited, pre-empts generate fun and profit.

Higher pre-empts

Opener has available two other pre-emptive bids, each following the same general principles as an opening three-bid.

1. An opening four-bid shows an excellent eight-card suit and a hand worth seven tricks not vulnerable, eight tricks vulnerable.

2. An opening five bid in a minor suit shows an excellent eight- or nine-card suit and a hand worth eight tricks not vulnerable, nine tricks vulnerable. (There is little sense to opening 5 ♡ or 5 ♠.)

These pre-empts are not as common as opening three-bids, but they conform to the same rule – good offense, poor defense. Similarly they take account of vulnerability: not vulnerable, the pre-emptor will be within three tricks of his bid; vulnerable, within two.

Quiz No. 8

1] You hold:
   ♠ A Q 10 8 7
   ♡ A K Q 3 2
   ◊ A Q J
   ♣ –
   What do you bid?

2] You hold:
   ♠ K J 8
   ♡ A Q 9 7
   ◊ A Q 5 4
   ♣ A Q
   What do you bid?

3] Partner opens 2 ♡ and you hold:
   ♠ 8 7
   ♡ J 7 6 3
   ◊ J 7 6
   ♣ J 6 5 2
   What is your response?

4] Partner opens 2 ◊ and you hold:
   ♠ 7
   ♡ A Q 6 5 4
   ◊ J 8 7
   ♣ 10 9 8 6
   What is your response?

5] Partner opens 2 NT and you hold:

♠ Q J 8
♥ A J 7 4
♦ K 8 7
♣ 10 9 8

What do you respond?

6] You deal yourself:

♠ K 5
♥ Q 10 8 7 6 4 2
♦ K 7
♣ 9 8

What do you bid?

7] You deal yourself:

♠ 7
♥ A K Q J 7 3 2
♦ 9 7
♣ 9 8 6

Vulnerable, what do you bid?

8] As dealer, you hold:

♠ 10
♥ K Q 10 9 7 6 4 2
♦ 7
♣ K 4 2

Not vulnerable, what do you bid?

9] As dealer, you hold:

♠ –
♥ J 7
♦ 4 2
♣ A Q J 9 8 7 6 3 2

Not vulnerable, what is your bid?

10] Partner opens 3 ♥ not vulnerable and you hold:

♠ A K 7 6
♥ 5
♦ A 7 6 5
♣ A K 8 2

What do you respond?

Answers to Quiz No. 9

1] **2 ♠**. Your hand is worth 25 points, more than enough for a forcing two-bid. With two five-card suits, start with the higher ranking.

2] **2 NT**. A minimum for this powerful but non-forcing bid (22–24).

3] **2 NT**. With such a weak hand, your first duty is to warn partner by giving the negative response. On the next round show your heart support.

4] **2 ♡**. A natural, positive response (6 points or more) forcing to game.

5] **6 NT**. Combining assets you know you own a minimum of 33 points which is the "magic number" for a small slam.

6] **Pass**. The hearts are too weak and you have too much defensive potential outside the heart suit to pre-empt. Maintain discipline.

7] **3 ♡**. Ideal. (Not vulnerable you might open **4 ♡**. Normally this shows an eight-card suit, but, more important, you have the perfect pre-empt pattern and you are within three tricks of your bid.)

8] **4 ♡**. The hand is worth about seven winners and the pattern is suitable for a pre-empt.

9] **5 ♣**. Just about the only way to describe this freak hand.

10] **4 ♡** – not 3 NT. This is a tricky one. The problem with 3 NT is that you might be unable to reach partner's hand to use the hearts. You could have to drive out the ♡ **A** or ♡ **K** and find that partner has no honor card on the side to use for re-entry. But in ♡ the pre-emptor's hand can be reached by trumping a side suit.

Lesson **10:** **competitive bidding**

About half of the time either you or your partner will open the bidding; the other half, one of the opponents will make the first bid. When the opponents begin the auction and you decide to compete, you are entering the area of defensive bidding. Defensive bids are made either in the hope of outbidding the opener's side and reaching a makeable contract; or, as a means of indicating the defense to an eventual contract played by the opponents; or, finding a profitable sacrifice bid. Occasionally, there is a defensive bid which is obstructive in nature, such as a pre-empt. But what is common to all good defensive bidding is a method of competing safely against a known strong hand (the opening bid).

Basically, there are two types of defensive bids: the *overcall* and the *take-out double*.

Overcalls

An overcall (literally, the call over an opening) shows at least five cards in the suit bid and trick-winning strength that depends on the level and the vulnerability, with a maximum of about 17 points. An overcall at the one-level (1 ♢ by the opener - 1 ♡) requires less strength than overcalling at the two-level (1 ♡ by the opener - 2 ♢). Valued in Point Count, a one-level overcall generally may be made on 10 points, while at the two-level the overcall starts at a minimum opening bid (13 points). In deciding close cases the vulnerability becomes a factor, as does suit quality. Winners are a better guide to overcalls than point count.

For instance:

♠ A K J 9 6
♡ 8
♢ 10 9 8 2
♣ 10 9 7

Your right hand opponent opens the bidding 1 ♡. Holding 10 points (including 2 distributional points) you have a borderline 1 ♠ overcall. Not vulnerable, with excellent suit quality, make the overcall. Vulnerable it is more prudent to pass. Suppose your opponent opens 1 ♠ and you hold:

♠ Q 7
♡ K J 7 4 2
♢ A J 6 2
♣ J 8

To overcall in your longest suit you must go to the two-level, so your 14-point hand (12 HCP plus 1 for each doubleton heart) is a borderline case. Here you should pass, even not vulnerable, because your suit quality is only fair. Change the hand slightly to:

♠ 7 2
♡ K Q J 7 4
♢ A J 6 2
♣ J 8

This hand is worth a 2 ♡ overcall, even vulnerable, because of the concentrated heart holding.

The safety factor

The reason an overcall should be based on a long, sound suit (exception: 1 NT overcall shows 16–18 points, balanced distribution) is to provide some measure of safety. Often the overcaller is competing against the opponents' greater high-card strength; to compensate he needs distributional assets.

Otherwise he may suffer stiff penalties when the opponents double him. This consideration is particularly true when both opener and responder have shown strength, as in 1 ♠ by opener - 2 ♣ by responder (second hand passing in between). Suppose you are in fourth seat and hold:

> ♠ Q J 6
> ♡ K 7
> ◇ A 9 8 6 4 2
> ♣ Q 10

This hand counts to 14 points (12 HCP + 2 for the doubletons), but it is far too dangerous to overcall 2 ◇. Your left-hand opponent has announced an opening bid, your right-hand opponent has shown 10 points or more by bidding a new suit at a higher level. What does that leave for partner? The answer is practically nothing, and your hand is not worth enough tricks on its own. An acceptable 2 ◇ overcall on this auction is a hand like:

> ♠ 4
> ♡ K Q 6
> ◇ K Q 10 9 7 5 3
> ♣ 9 7

This hand should produce at least six tricks on its own, and it is less likely to encounter a penalty double from an opponent loaded in diamonds.

Decide for yourself which of the following hands represents an acceptable overcall, vulnerable. Assume the bidding to be 1 ◇ - Pass (by partner) - 1 ♡ - ???

a]	b]	c]
♠ Q J 10 8 6 2	♠ A 4	♠ K Q 2
♡ 8 7	♡ 9 8 7 3	♡ 9 8
◇ 3	◇ K 8	◇ 10 2
♣ A J 8 2	♣ Q J 9 8 7	♣ A Q 10 9 7 3

Hand a) is a sound 1 ♠ overcall; hand b) should pass; hand c) is an acceptable 2 ♣ bid. Note that the opponents' bidding in this sequence is not necessarily strong. The 1 ♡ response could be made on as few as 6 points. Thus, there is a reasonable chance of finding partner with a helpful hand.

Responding to overcalls

The responder to an overcall assumes partner has a minimum of a five-card suit, so he can feel free to raise with three-card support. A single raise shows 6–9 points, just like the raise of an opening bid. Without support or a decent long suit of his own, responder should pass unless he has at least 9 points. The overcaller has at most 17 points, putting game out of reach if responder has 8 or fewer. Why, then, should responder raise with only 6 points? The reason is that an eight-card fit provides safety, and the advantage of raising the level of the bidding is that it prevents the opponents from buying a cheap, easy-to-make contract.

Responding with stronger hands

When responder has 10–12 points plus support, he should offer a jump raise. This is not forcing but invites the overcaller to continue with extra values. With a hand in this point range but without support, responder can bid a new suit holding at least five, or bid 1 NT if he can guard the opposing suit(s). The change-of-suit response is not forcing; if responder wishes to force he must either jump in a new suit or make a *cue-bid*.

Cue-bids

A cue-bid is a bid in the opponent's suit, such as 1 ◇ - 1 ♠ (by partner) - Pass - 2 ◇. Cue-bidding is an advanced topic, but you should know that a cue-bid is a strong, general direction move that is forcing and invites a game contract. Note that a cue-bid is available only in competitive auctions. When responder to an overcall holds 13 points or more, he will usually jump in a new suit (forcing), jump to game in the overcaller's suit (with support), or cue-bid (forcing) if he needs more information.

Assume the bidding has proceded 1 ♡ - 2 ♣ (by partner) - Pass - ??? What should you respond with each of the following hands?

d]	♠ J 8 7	e]	♠ Q 5 2	f]	♠ A 6 4
	♡ A 4		♡ K 8 7 5 3		♡ 10 9
	◇ 10 9 3 2		◇ J 8 7 6		◇ K Q 9 5 3 2
	♣ Q 6 4 3		♣ 9		♣ J 10

g]	♠ K J 7	h]	♠ 10 9
	♡ Q 6 4 3		♡ K J 7 5
	◇ Q J 9		◇ A J 5 3
	♣ J 10 8		♣ A J 6

Hand d) should bid 3 ♣, 8 points with club support (7 HCP + 1 for the doubleton heart). Hand e) should pass. Bidding probably will make matters worse. Hand f) should respond 2 ◇. Bid a new suit only with a constructive hand (9 points or more). Hand g) should respond 2 NT. Again, a forward going bid is constructive. Hand h) should bid 2 ♡, a cue-bid. (It is only coincidence that the hand includes heart length. The same bid would be made with the spade and heart holdings reversed.) 3 NT is a likely contract if partner can bid spades. Since an overcaller may have two suits, a probing bid is in order.

Pre-emptive overcalls

It is modern practice that a jump overcall shows a long suit and a weak hand, much like an opening pre-empt. After a 1 ♡ opening, an overcall of 2 ♠, 3 ♣, or 3 ◇ is considered pre-emptive because each bid skips one level. (The fourth seat defender may also use the device.) The requirements are the same as for an opening pre-empt (see Lesson 8). In brief, at the three-level the jump overcall shows a strong seven-card suit with little defensive trick-taking potential; at the two-level the same type of hand is expected but only a six-card suit. Naturally, when vulnerable the long suit must be of better quality.

The purpose of the bid is to obstruct the opponents from communicating successfully. With favorable vulnerability, partner can add to the pre-emption, perhaps locating a profitable sacrifice or even a makeable game. The tactics for responding to jump overcalls are basically the same as responding to opening pre-empts. (Again, review Lesson 9).

Assume you are in second seat, neither side vulnerable, and the opener bids 1 ◇. What would you bid with each of the following hands?

i] ♠ 9 7
    ♡ K Q 10 9 6 2
    ◇ 7
    ♣ J 9 8 2

j] ♠ 10
    ♡ K 7 6
    ◇ 4 3
    ♣ K J 10 9 7 6 2

k] ♠ A J 9 7 5 3
    ♡ A J 6
    ◇ 8 7
    ♣ 6 4

l] ♠ A K J 10 6 4 2
    ♡ 5
    ◇ 8 7
    ♣ J 10 2

Hand i) should overcall 2 ♡. Ideal. Hand j) is a good example of a 3 ♣ jump overcall. Hand k) should simply bid 1 ♠. It has too much defensive potential for a pre-empt. Hand l) should make a double jump overcall of 3 ♠; 2 ♠ shows only a six-card suit and doesn't do justice to this hand. Make the maximum pre-empt at the first opportunity.

As the last example indicates, jump overcalls come in different sizes. With an eight-card suit and the appropriate hand, a triple jump overcall is advisable (1 ♡ - 4 ♠). With wild distribution, be a nuisance to the opponents! Properly used, the weak jump overcall will pay handsome dividends.

There is one wise precaution, however. Be certain that your partner agrees to play a single jump overcall as weak! Not long ago, it was assumed that jump overcalls showed considerable power. If your partner learned it this way he may treat your intended pre-empt as an 18-point hand. Get your signals straight before you start to play – it's less expensive that way.

Take-out doubles

Often you will hold a hand with which you wish to compete, but one which is not suitable for an overcall. For instance, your right hand opponent opens the bidding with 1 ◇ and you hold:

♠ K J 6 4
♡ Q J 10 4
◇ 6
♣ A Q 3 2

An overcall promises at least a five-card suit, and even if you decided to ignore this, which suit would you pick? Partner might fit either or both of the suits you neglected. Yet you don't want to pass with a hand that is so promising for offense. The solution is to double, which carries the message: "Partner, I wish to compete but I need your help in deciding on our best fit." In other words, you have good support for all the unbid suits, and you are giving partner his choice (asking him to *take out* your double to his longest suit).

Since partner of the take-out doubler may be forced to show his best suit at the two-level, the double should promise at least the strength of a minimum opening bid (13 points plus). The take-out double may also be used by the player in the fourth seat: 1 ♣ - Pass - 1 ♡ - DOUBLE shows support for diamonds and spades, the unbid suits. The take-out double is a way of bidding two or three suits "simultaneously." Whereas the overcall tends to put all the partnership's eggs in one basket, the take-out double's great virtue is its flexibility. Responder is immediately presented with a choice of two or three suits to support and knows that the doubler has a good hand.

The following hands are all suitable take-out doubles of a 1 ♠ opening.

m]		n]		o]	
♠	10 4	♠	4	♠	–
♡	K 9 7 4	♡	A Q 4 2	♡	Q J 7 6
◇	A K 7	◇	K J 9 8 7	◇	K Q J 7
♣	K 10 9 6	♣	Q 10 8	♣	A Q 10 7 2

Note that the take-out doubler should always be short in the opponent's suit(s). While the ideal take-out double contains at least four-card support for each unbid suit, frequently the doubler will make use of the bid with only three-card support. But in these cases it is preferable that the three-card suit be a minor. The double of a major suit usually promises four cards in the "other" major.

Responding to a take-out double

Responses to the take-out double depend somewhat on what the opponents do. If the bidding has gone:

1 ◇ - Double - Pass - ???

doubler's partner is expected to bid, even with a very weak hand. In contrast, if the bidding proceeds:

1 ◇ - Double - 2 ◇ - ???

the doubler's partner should pass with a weak hand. If the intervening opponent passes over the take-out double, responder is obliged to bid (with one exception, which we will discuss in a moment). If right-hand opponent bids (or redoubles), responder is released from his obligation to bid and does so only with a useful hand.

With hands of fewer than 10 points, responder makes a minimum take-out in his longest unbid suit. If he has equal length in a major and a minor, he bids the major.

With 10 points or more, responder must make a strong bid to invite game. He can jump in his longest suit, even if it is only a four-card suit, or, if his hand is so strong as to insist on game (13 points plus) he may decide to cue-bid to explore the best fit. Some examples:

The bidding has gone 1 ◇ - Double - Pass - ???

a]		b]		c]	
♠ J765		♠ Q873		♠ K863	
♡ 643		♡ A3		♡ AJ42	
◇ 542		◇ 987		◇ 53	
♣ 872		♣ A764		♣ AQ2	
Bid 1 ♠		**Bid 2 ♠**		**Bid 2 ◇**	

Note that it is not dangerous to jump in a four-card suit when responding to the take-out double; you are really supporting one of the suits partner has implicitly bid. Also note that you mustn't pass out of fright; e.g., hand a). If you did pass, the opener could pass and play a final contract of 1 ◇ doubled, probably making with several costly doubled overtricks.

The only occasion when you pass partner's take-out double (assuming right hand opponent has passed) is with extraordinary length and strength in opener's suit. For instance, you might pass partner's take-out double of 1 ◇ holding:

♠ A 4
♡ J 9
◇ Q J 10 9 2
♣ 9 8 7 6

Here you are happy to defend 1 ◇ doubled because you have several trump tricks, while partner can help take care of the unbid suits. Change your hand slightly to

♠ A 4
♡ J 9 6
◇ Q J 5 4 2
♣ 9 8 7

and your best response is 1 NT. This denies four-card support for one of partner's "silently bid" suits and shows strength in the opponent's suit, yet not quite enough to defend a low-level doubled contract. A jump response to 2 NT would show the same hand pattern and about 10–12 points, inviting game. With a still stronger hand responder could jump to 3 NT after the take-out double.

The take-out double has one more important function. Since the overcall is limited to 17 points, and a jump overcall shows a hand that is weaker, not stronger, than a normal overcall, how does a defender describe an overcall of more than 17 points? The answer is to employ the take-out double, then bid the long suit over partner's response. For example:

♠ A Q 10 9 7 3
♡ K Q 4
◇ A Q
♣ 7 6

Right hand opponent opens 1 ◇. A 1 ♠ overcall doesn't do justice to this hand. Instead, double, and if partner bids, say, 2 ♣, rebid 2 ♠ to show a hand too strong to make a simple overcall.

The take-out double can be used at higher levels of the auction. Opener bids 3 ♣ pre-emptively and you are in second seat holding:

$$\begin{array}{l}
♠ \text{ K Q 7 6} \\
♡ \text{ A K 4 2} \\
◇ \text{ A J 8} \\
♣ \text{ 9 7}
\end{array}$$

You should double for take-out. Naturally, since the level is higher, the doubler needs a better hand than for doubling a one-level opening. Responder may be forced to take out at the three-level or (over a 3 ♠ opening) even higher.

The responding principles basically remain the same, except that responder will more readily pass with modest strength in opener's suit, thereby converting the take-out double into a *penalty double*. (High level contracts are easier to defeat.)

Distinguishing between take-out and penalty doubles

This brings us to the final topic of this lesson: how to distinguish a take-out double from a penalty double. The player who says "double" is not permitted to add any modifying words, such as "take-out" or "penalty." The way to distinguish between these two types of doubles is summarized in the chart that follows:

	Take-out double	Penalty double
Level-	Usually below game	Usually at game (or higher)
Partner-	Has passed once, or made no bid	Has already bid or doubled

To help distinguish, compare some examples of each kind of double.

1 ♡ - Pass - 2 ♡ - Double (Take-out)
1 ♠ - Pass - 2 ◇ - Double (Take-out)
1 ◇ - Pass - 1 ♡ - Pass
2 ♡ - Double (Take-out)
1NT - Pass - 2 ♡ - Double (Take-out)

1 ♠ - Pass - 2 ♠ - Pass
4 ♠ - Double (Penalty)
1 ♠ - Pass - 2 ♣ - 2 ◇
2 ♠ - Double (Penalty)
1 ♣ - 1 ♡ - Pass - 4 ♡
Pass - Pass - Double (Penalty)

It is rare to overrule a penalty double by taking out, just as it is rare to overrule a take-out double by passing for penalties. Treating partner's doubles as he intended them is an important illustration of why bridge is a partnership game.

Quiz No. 10

1] In second seat, your right hand opponent opens 1 ♠. What do you bid holding:
  ♠ J 10 8
  ♡ A Q 3
  ◇ A J 7
  ♣ K 6 4 3

2] In fourth seat, the bidding has gone: 1 ♣ - Pass - 1 ♠ - ???
  What do you bid with:
  ♠ Q 5
  ♡ A Q 9 8 7 4
  ◇ K Q 4 3
  ♣ 7

3] Your partner overcalls a 1 ◇ opening with 1 ♡ (next player passes). What do you bid holding:
  ♠ A J 6 5
  ♡ Q 5
  ◇ K 9 8
  ♣ J 10 9 7

4]   You hold:
     ♠ 5
     ♡ K J 10 9 8 3
     ◇ Q 6 5 3
     ♣ 8 2

     Neither side is vulnerable and right-hand opponent opens
     1 ♣. What do you bid?

5]   In second seat, right hand opponent opens 1 ♡. What do
     you bid with:
     ♠ Q J 7 6
     ♡ 6 5
     ◇ K Q 5 3
     ♣ A J 7

6]   In fourth seat, the bidding has gone:
       1 ♡ - Pass - 2 ◇ - ???
     What do you bid with:
     ♠ K J 7 2
     ♡ 9 8
     ◇ Q 7
     ♣ K J 10 8 2

7]   Left hand opponent opens 1 ♡ - partner doubles - right hand
     opponent passes. What do you bid with:
     ♠ K 8 7
     ♡ 7 6
     ◇ A K 8 7 2
     ♣ 9 8 2

8]   You hold:
     ♠ A 8 7
     ◇ 8 7 2
     ◇ K 10 8 6
     ♣ J 9 8

     Left hand opponent opens 3 ◇ - partner doubles - right hand
     opponent passes. What do you bid?

9]   You hold:
     ♠ K Q 6
     ♡ Q J 10 9 6
     ◇ 10 9 7
     ♣ 10 9

     Right hand opponent opens 1 ♡ - you pass - left hand
     opponent bids 2 ♡ - partner doubles - right hand opponent
     passes. What do you bid now?

10] You hold:
    ♠ 8 7 6 4
    ♡ K Q J 7 4
    ◇ –
    ♣ Q 9 8 2
The bidding has gone: 1 ♠ at your left - 3 ♣ by partner -
4 ♠ at your right. With both sides vulnerable, what do you
bid?

Answers to Quiz No. 10

1] **Pass.** You are slightly too weak to overcall 1 NT (16–18) and
the hand does not have enough four-card suits for a take-out
double. Your hand is well suited for defense, so be patient
and pass.

2] **2 ♡.** A minimum two-level overcall. A double would not
describe your heart length.

3] **1 NT.** A natural, forward going, but non-forcing bid.

4] **2 ♡.** An ideal weak jump overcall.

5] **Double.** Gives partner the most options to select a suit.

6] **Pass.** Although your distribution is right for a take-out
double, the hand is too weak. Remember that both opponents have bid strongly, leaving little for partner.

7] **3 ◇.** You must distinguish between this useful hand and a
worthless hand with which you would be compelled to bid
2 ◇.

8] **3 NT.** A pass, converting partner's take-out double to
penalty, is possible but too risky. (If the 3 ◇ doubled
contract makes, it is a game.) You expect to make 3 NT
since partner will cover the other three suits.

9] **Pass.** This is the right time to convert partner's take-out
double to penalty. On defense your hand is worth four tricks
against hearts; all partner has to do is supply two or more
and he has promised opening bid strength.

10] **5 ♣.** Partner's vulnerable weak jump overcall indicates your
side combined will have no trump losers, no diamonds (your
void), one one heart, and probably only one spade – perhaps
none, since the opponents have apparently found a fit.
Situations like this stress the value of counting winners and
losers on distributionally wild hands.

Lesson 11: card play

The subject of declarer play could provide enough material for an entire book; the same can be said for defense. What we will do in this chapter is guide you through four basic deals, pointing out general principles that can be applied to many of the situations you are likely to encounter. In each deal assume declarer is sitting South. Follow the play from that vantage point while taking note of what the defenders are doing. It may be helpful to actually lay out the cards to see how a hand develops.

DEAL NO. 1

North
♠ K Q 10 6 4
♡ K Q 2
♢ 10 9 5
♣ 7 3

West
♠ 7 3
♡ A 6 4
♢ K Q J 8 2
♣ 6 5 4

East
♠ 9 8 5 2
♡ J 9 5
♢ 7 3
♣ J 10 9 8

South
♠ A J
♡ 10 8 7 3
♢ A 6 4
♣ A K Q 2

Contract: 3 NT   Opening lead: ♢ K

South is declarer at 3 NT, reached by the bidding:

South	West	North	East
1 NT	Pass	3 ♠	Pass
3 NT	Pass	Pass	Pass

West's opening lead is the ◇ K because he wants to establish his longest suit; he leads the ◇ K to show he holds a sequence of honor cards.

The dummy is now exposed by North and South can begin to plan the play. At notrump, declarer should generally turn to his long suit(s) for tricks – for the same reason, the defenders try to establish their long suit. On this deal declarer's most productive asset is dummy's five-card spade suit; since he owns all the spade honors between the two hands, the suit is worth five tricks.

At notrump declarer should count winners, while at suit play we will see that it is preferable to count losers. We have already counted five winners in spades; since we require nine tricks to make our contract we need four more winners. On this deal the winners are easy to spot: the ◇ A plus the ♣ A, ♣ K and ♣ Q – the needed four winners. Thus, we are in a position to make our contract by taking the nine winners that are already established.

Returning our attention to the opening lead, as declarer South has the option of winning the first, second, or third round of diamonds. Since we cannot lose our ◇ A in notrump and since we can comfortably cope if the defenders shift suits, it is good practice to *hold up* our ace, allowing the ◇ K to win the first trick. West stays with his plan to establish diamond tricks by continuing with the ◇ Q. Note that he must play an honor to prevent dummy's ◇ 9 from winning a cheap trick. Declarer holds up a second time, winning the third round of diamonds as East discards his lowest heart. Observe the potential advantage of holding up the ◇ A (although it doesn't happen to gain on this particular deal). One opponent is now out of diamonds, so that if declarer lost the lead to East the defenders could not immediately pursue their attack.

Declarer now starts his long suit, and here he must take care to *unblock*. This is generally accomplished by leading the highest honor from the short hand. In our deal, this means playing ♠ A the first time we play the suit. The best way to learn unblocking is to notice what happens when we fail to unblock. Suppose declarer starts by leading ♠ J. Everyone follows with a low card. Next declarer leads ♠ A. He is still in his own hand, but the remaining spades are in dummy and he has no way to reach them. If he tries a heart, West rises with the ♡ A and takes his two remaining diamonds, setting the contract one trick.

With correct unblocking technique, the hand is smooth sailing. Declarer leads ♠ A and continues with ♠ J. Dummy *overtakes* ♠ J with ♠ Q so that the suit can be continued. Declarer cashes the rest of dummy's spades, then returns to his hand with a club to take his three top winners there. The defenders can gain the lead only after declarer has won nine tricks.

DEAL NO. 2

```
                       North
                       ♠ K Q 4
                       ♡ J 9 5
                       ◇ A 7 3
                       ♣ A Q 8 2
         West                            East
         ♠ 8 2                           ♠ 10 9 6
         ♡ A 7 3                         ♡ K Q 10 6 4
         ◇ K Q J 4                       ◇ 10 9 6
         ♣ 10 9 6 5                      ♣ 7 3
                       South
                       ♠ A J 7 5 3
                       ♡ 8 2
                       ◇ 8 5 2
                       ♣ K J 4
```

Contract: 4 ♠   Opening Lead: ◇ K

South has arrived in 4 ♠ by this auction:

North	East	South	West
1NT	Pass	3 ♠	Pass
4 ♠	Pass	Pass	Pass

West attacks in his strongest suit, leading the top card of his honor sequence. In a suit contract, declarer counts his losers before he makes his plan. On this deal declarer is faced with two losing hearts (the third round can be trumped) and two losing diamonds, and no losers in either clubs or spades. This is a total of four losers, one more than declarer can afford, so he must look for a way to dispose of one loser. Fortunately, dummy's long suit (clubs) can be used to provide coverage of a loser in declarer's hand. By playing four rounds of clubs, on the fourth round declarer will be void and have the opportunity to discard a red-suit loser. But if declarer plays clubs before trumps, the defense can ruff one of the high clubs with a low spade. Therefore, the proper strategy is to draw the opposing trumps; then play clubs without fear of a ruff.

Regarding the opening lead, declarer should not hold up, because in a suit contract there is a risk of losing dummy's ace to a ruff should East happen to have a singleton diamond. Declarer wins dummy's ◇ A and starts to draw trumps. Unblocking technique is called for, so ♠ K and ♠ Q are played first, then ♠ 4 to declarer's ♠ A. (Declarer should always keep track of how many trumps have been played; here, each opponent has followed to two rounds and East has followed to the third round. Five opposing trumps have been played, and originally five were outstanding, so all the trumps have been drawn. Familiarize yourself with this *counting* process; you will have occasion to use it again and again.)

Having drawn the opponent's trumps, declarer plays clubs, and he unblocks them by first cashing ♣ K and ♣ J from his hand. Next, he leads the ♣ 4 to dummy's ♣ Q, and on ♣ A declarer discards either a heart or a diamond. He concedes the remaining three red-suit losers and claims his contract.

DEAL NO. 3   *North*
                                  ♠ Q J 10
                                  ♡ A 6 4
                                  ◇ 6 5 4
West   ♣ J 10 8 2
♠ 10 9 5 3   *East*
♡ Q J 10 5 2   ♠ K 8 7 2
◇ 8 3   ♡ 8 7 3
♣ K Q 9   ◇ A 10 9
                                  South   ♣ 6 5 4
                                  ♠ A 6 4
                                  ♡ K 9
                                  ◇ K Q J 7 2
                                  ♣ A 7 3

Contract: 3 NT   Opening Lead: ♡ **Q**

Playing again at notrump (1 NT by South - 2 NT by North - 3 NT by South), declarer should count his winners. In immediate tricks he has one spade, two hearts, and one club. By establishing diamonds (driving out ◇ A), he has good prospects for four more winners. He must hope that the five missing cards in the suit split 3–2, which will happen more than two-thirds of the time. This will bring his trick total to eight, one short of his contract. That extra trick can come from playing ♠ Q from dummy and trapping East's ♠ K. This type of play is known as a *finesse* and is commonly employed in all contracts. But this finesse will only work if ♠ K is with East and the suit is led from the dummy, which means that declarer must manage his *entries* carefully. Dummy has only one sure entry card – ♡ A – and this must be conserved until declarer is ready to take the spade finesse. Since it is generally correct in notrump to establish long suit tricks first, declarer wins the opening ♡ Q lead (top card of an honor sequence) with ♡ K in his hand and plays a high diamond.

East wins the trick with his ◇ A and returns a heart. Playing back the suit that partner originally led is usually sound policy on defense. Here East reasons that partner would attack with his best suit at notrump, so that even though ♡ A is still visible in dummy, it is right to return a heart to establish opening leader's long suit. Suit establishment works for the defenders, too.

Declarer takes dummy's ♡ A and is at the crossroads. He is in dummy for the last time, so he mustn't waste this opportunity by leading diamonds to cash his established tricks. Diamonds can be led from his hand with equal effect, but spades can only be led effectively from the dummy. Therefore, declarer plays ♠ Q from the table and crosses his fingers. If West has ♠ K along with a long heart suit, the contract is doomed. But if ♠ K is with East – a 50 % chance – the finesse will succeed and West's established heart suit will go to waste. On this deal, the spade finesse can be repeated by leading ♠ J if East fails to cover ♠ Q; in either case declarer scores three spade tricks. Combined with two hearts, four diamonds, and one club this produces an overtrick at 3 NT. Accurate play (plus a little luck) justifies aggressive bidding.

DEAL NO. **4**

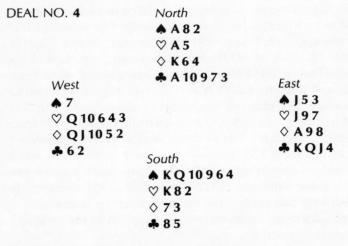

North
♠ A 8 2
♡ A 5
◇ K 6 4
♣ A 10 9 7 3

West
♠ 7
♡ Q 10 6 4 3
◇ Q J 10 5 2
♣ 6 2

East
♠ J 5 3
♡ J 9 7
◇ A 9 8
♣ K Q J 4

South
♠ K Q 10 9 6 4
♡ K 8 2
◇ 7 3
♣ 8 5

Contract: **4 ♠**   Opening Lead: ◇ **Q**

After an aggressive bidding sequence, as South are declarer at 4 ♠. Incidentally, as skill and confidence in your declarer play grows, you will become more willing to take some chances (sensible ones) in the bidding. In the long run this will be to your benefit.

In a suit contract you remember to count your losers. You are entitled to assume no spade losers, two possible diamond losers, and one club loser. This does not leave room for any heart losers if you wish to make your contract. This means you must take care of the low third heart in your hand.

The opening lead is significant; it is bad news for the declarer. You remember that an honor lead is usually the top card of a sequence, which places ◇ J with West and ◇ A with East. This means that dummy's ◇ K cannot win a trick. But if ◇ A had been with West, dummy's ◇ K would have been worth a trick and declarer would have had only one diamond loser. Let us say that declarer plays low from dummy on the opening lead. East should *signal* with ◇ 9. On defense the play of an unnecessarily high spot card encourages partner to continue the suit; the play of a very low spot card discourages. This is another very common signalling technique.

West duly continues the diamonds and declarer trumps the third round. He starts to draw trumps by playing low to dummy's ♠ A; then a spade to his ♠ K. On this second round he notes that West *discards* (a low heart). Counting trumps, he realizes that one is still outstanding. However, he must resist the temptation to draw it. One more round of spades will exhaust both East's and the dummy's trumps, which means that declarer will no longer be able to trump his losing heart on the table. And as we already calculated, if declarer loses a heart trick he loses his contract.

Therefore, declarer leaves one trump outstanding and plays ♡ 2 to ♡ A (unblocking), ♡ 5 to his ♡ K, and then the losing ♡ 8, which he trumps with dummy's carefully conserved low spade. Next, ♣ A and a second round of clubs. Declarer can trump any return and then play his high spade, drawing East's ♠ J and claiming the contract. On deals like this, and there are many of them, there is a slight risk in leaving trump(s) outstanding, but it is suicide to draw them and be faced with losers elsewhere. Remember, trumping losers in the dummy is one of the major advantages of playing in a suit contract.

As we mentioned earlier, this chapter is by no means a complete treatment of card play. (Readers who wish to press ahead have many books on the subject to choose from.*) However, by studying these deals and understanding the principles, you will develop a good feel for how the game of bridge is played.

*Including Charles Goren's monumental "Play and Defense," Doubleday.

Lesson **12:**   **Fine points**

This section of the book is not "required reading" in the sense that you will be able to begin to play bridge without it. Still, we will cover two bids that are both very useful and very commonly played.

In bridge, a *convention* is a special coded bid that does not mean what it sounds like it should mean. Ordinarily when a player bids clubs he has clubs, but if, as some play, an opening bid of 2 ♣ shows a strong hand without saying anything about the club suit, that 2 ♣ bid is a convention.

Two virtually standard conventions are *Blackwood* and *Stayman*. You will undoubtedly play in games where partner will want to use them, so if you learn these conventions not only will you be an accommodating partner but you will also make the most out of many more hands.

Blackwood 4 NT Convention

The Blackwood convention is used in slam bidding. Specifically, when bidding toward a slam, a bid of 4 NT asks partner how many aces he has. Responder replies in the following manner:

Holding 0 or 4 aces, respond 5 ♣.
Holding 1 ace, respond 5 ◇.

113

Holding 2 aces, respond 5 ♡.
Holding 3 aces, respond 5 ♠.

(Don't worry about the dual meaning of the 5 ♣ response. The previous bidding and your own hand will make clear what is meant.)

If the 4 NT bidder wants to inquire about the number of kings partner holds, (at the same time guaranteeing that the partnership owns all the aces), he continues the convention by bidding 5 NT. Responses follow the same pattern as the aces, except that all bids occur at the six-level. (6 ♣ shows 0 or 4 kings, 6 ♢ = 1 king, etc.)

That's basic Blackwood. The reason for the convention is to avoid slam contracts missing two aces. The convention also helps the partnership diagnose good grand slams by indicating the presence of all the aces and all the kings. It is simple to remember since the key bid, 4 NT, is rarely useful as a natural bid. (3 NT is enough for game.) And the responses follow a step pattern: the cheapest response (5 ♣ shows the fewest number of aces or the most), the next step up the ladder (5 ♢) shows one, the step after that (5 ♡) two, and the highest step (5 ♠) three.

A bit of advice about Blackwood: don't use the 4 NT bid until you have first found a sound trump suit, and don't use the convention unless you feel that a five-level contract is very safe. It's a shame to go down one at 5 ♠ and thereby toss a game out the window.

A final warning about Blackwood based on observation: too many players overrule partner's final decision. The player who starts Blackwood becomes the captain of the partnership (for that one hand). If the captain asks for aces, receives the reply, and decides to sign off at the five-level, responder should respect that decision. After all, the 4 NT bidder may have discovered that two aces are missing. Yet we have seen many a responder carry on to a hopeless slam because he "liked my hand." Only the rare instance of a void can condone overruling the captain.

The Stayman 2 ♣ Convention

The Stayman convention is used after a 1 NT or 2 NT opening. Specifically, it is a bid of 2 ♣ (or 3 ♣ after 2 NT) by responder asking the opener if he has a four-card major. With one major opener names it; with both four-card majors he bids 2 ♠ (responding in the higher-ranking four-card suit). With no four-card major, opener bids 2 ◊.

The purpose of Stayman is to locate 4–4 major suit fits. After a 1 NT opening, 2 ◊, 2 ♡, and 2 ♠ are all weak bids showing at least a five-card suit. All suit responses at the three-level are at least five cards and forcing to game. What, therefore, does responder bid with a hand like this facing a 1 NT opening?

♠ Q 10 8 5
♡ A J 6 2
◊ K 8 7 3
♣ 9

By combining points, responder knows he wants to be in game, but which game? This is a spot for the Stayman convention. Responder bids 2 ♣ (no relation to club length) to see if opener can fit one of the major suits. If he finds a fit he bids game in the major (where responder's hand grows in value to 13 points – 3 for the singleton). If there is no major-suit fit (2 ◊ rebid by opener), responder bids 3 NT and has lost nothing by investigating.

To use Stayman, responder is usually interested in reaching game, meaning he has 8 points or more. Holding:

♠ Q J 6 4
♡ 8 3
◊ A 5 4
♣ J 10 8 6

it is proper to bid 2 ♣ opposite a 1 NT opening. If opener bids 2 ♠ responder will raise to 3 ♠, inviting game. If opener bids 2 ◊ or 2 ♡ responder will rebid 2 NT, inviting game in notrump if opener has more than a minimum. As long as the Stayman bidder has a sensible rebid after any response, it is proper to use the convention.

Using the Stayman convention creates one minor problem, easily solved. Suppose you pick up ♠ 7 3   ♡ 8 6 4 ◇ J 10 ♣ Q J 8 5 3 2 and partner opens 1 NT. You wish to play a part score contract in your long suit, but a bid of 2 ♣ no longer shows clubs. Since jumping to the three-level is forcing, the solution is to bid 2 ♣ (which partner will interpret as Stayman) and then follow with a rebid of 3 ♣. Partner now gets the message and passes, playing you for a weak hand with long clubs.

Stayman after a 2 NT opening follows exactly the same pattern of rebids. Since exploration begins at the three-level, responder is forcing the partnership to game. Stayman can be used to explore for slam as well. Assume partner opens 2 NT (22–24) and you hold:

♠ K J 8 7 3
♡ K J 8 5
◇ Q 7
♣ 10 7.

Begin with 3 ♣ to check for the majors. Let's say partner responds 3 ◇ (no four-card major). That eliminates the chance of a heart fit, but a spade fit is still possible. Bid 3 ♠. This bid is forcing (since Stayman over 2 NT forces to game) and by inference must show a five-card suit. (After a negative response to a Stayman inquiry you would abandon the majors with only four.) Opener now raises to 4 ♠ holding three-card support; he rebids 3 NT with a doubleton. This sequence allows responder to choose the best slam (6 ♠ or 6 NT) after conducting a delicate investigation. Subtle communication through fine points like these help to make bridge a fascinating lifetime pursuit.